OUR
COSMIC
ANCESTRY
IN THE
STARS

"Our Cosmic Ancestry in the Stars is an excellent read! Professor Chandra Wickramasinghe, a pioneer of the theory of panspermia and cosmic biology, writes of the accumulating evidence that life populates all capable hosting places throughout the galaxy and the universe. The authors of the book conclude that our salvation as a species lies in the recognition and acknowledgment of our inalienable cosmic origins."

RUDY SCHILD, PH.D., EMERITUS ASTRONOMER AT THE HARVARD-SMITHSONIAN CENTER FOR ASTROPHYSICS

"This is a beautifully written book about our cosmic origins and will be understood by everyone wanting to learn more about the origins and further evolution of life on Earth. All the authors have been actively involved in assembling the hard scientific evidence for panspermia and communicating these important proofs to a wider audience. For the past 50 years Sir Fred Hoyle, Professor Chandra Wickramasinghe, and their many contemporary collaborators, such as Gensuke Tokoro, director of the Institute for the Study of Panspermia and Astrobiology (Gifu, Japan), are causing, through their untiring efforts, the second Copernican revolution. Thus 500 years after Copernicus, Galileo, Tycho Brahe, Kepler, then Newton displaced the Earth from the center of the universe, which heralded the birth of the Renaissance in medieval Europe, we are now witnessing an extraordinary rebirth in scientific thinking. We therefore live in revolutionary times. Life *did not originate* from nonliving elements on the early Earth as is commonly believed—as promulgated by the traditional neo-Darwinian theory of terrestrial evolution. It originated at some unknowable time in deep cosmic antiquity and has spread by panspermic infections and further evolution to all life-compatible habits—comets, moons, planets—throughout the universe."

EDWARD J. STEELE, PH.D.,
COAUTHOR OF *LAMARCK'S SIGNATURE*

"Chandra Wickramasinghe's central belief that basic microbial life in the universe could be very common and that it naturally spread across the galaxy is extended in this book to take on the topics of evolution itself and the future progress of humanity. Half a century after Neil Armstrong's 'one small step' on the moon, this book is timely, as the authors ponder key 'cosmic' questions about where we may have come from and what our future holds."

NICK SPALL, SPACE AND SCIENCE WRITER

"Everybody should read this brilliant book! It tells you the answers to many of the things that keep you awake at night. Ultimately, this is a book of hope, the hope of the universal prevalence of life and that we are all part of a cosmic community which has no ending. Read this book and see everything you thought you knew in a new and vital perspective."

ROBERT TEMPLE, AUTHOR OF *THE SPHINX MYSTERY*

OUR
COSMIC
ANCESTRY
IN THE
STARS

The Panspermia Revolution and the Origins of Humanity

Chandra Wickramasinghe, Ph.D.,
Kamala Wickramasinghe, MA,
and Gensuke Tokoro

Bear & Company
Rochester, Vermont

Bear & Company
One Park Street
Rochester, Vermont 05767
www.BearandCompanyBooks.com

Text stock is SFI certified

Bear & Company is a division of Inner Traditions International

Library of Congress Cataloging-in-Publication Data

Names: Wickramasinghe, Chandra, 1939- author. | Wickramasinghe, Kamala, author. | Tokoro, Gensuke, 1949- author.
Title: Our cosmic ancestry in the stars : the panspermia revolution and the origins of humanity / Chandra Wickramasinghe, Ph.D., Kamala Wickramasinghe, M.A., and Gensuke Tokoro.
Description: Rochester, Vermont : Bear & Company, [2019] | Includes bibliographical references and index.
Identifiers: LCCN 2018039458 (print) | LCCN 2018056525 (ebook) | ISBN 9781591433286 (pbk.) | ISBN 9781591433293 (ebook)
Subjects: LCSH: Life—Origin. | Exobiology. | Cosmic grains.
Classification: LCC QH325 .W5325 2019 (print) | LCC QH325 (ebook) | DDC 576.8/3—dc23
LC record available at https://lccn.loc.gov/2018039458

Printed and bound in the United States by Lake Book Manufacturing, Inc. The text stock is SFI certified. The Sustainable Forestry Initiative® program promotes sustainable forest management.

10 9 8 7 6 5 4 3 2 1

Text design and layout by Debbie Glogover
This book was typeset in Garamond Premier Pro with Insignia LT Std, Tide Sans and Gill Sans MT Pro used as display fonts

To send correspondence to the author of this book, mail a first-class letter to the author c/o Inner Traditions • Bear & Company, One Park Street, Rochester, VT 05767, and we will forward the communication, or contact Chandra Wickramasinghe directly at **www.profchandra.org**.

CONTENTS

PROLOGUE   Our Inalienable Link to the Cosmos   1

CHAPTER 1   Genesis of a Theory   4

CHAPTER 2   The Deepest Questions   18

CHAPTER 3   A Cosmic Creator?   25

CHAPTER 4   The Nature of Consciousness   34

CHAPTER 5   Viral Footprints in the Evolution to
             Homo sapiens sapiens   42

CHAPTER 6   Unbridled Greed—A Cosmic Imperative?   49

CHAPTER 7   Lessons from the Copernican Revolution   59

CHAPTER 8   East Is East and West Is West   70

CHAPTER 9   The Threat of Cometary Missiles   80

CHAPTER 10   A Historical Context   93

CHAPTER 11   So What if We Came from Space?   101

CHAPTER 12   The World of 2100   107

EPILOGUE   The New Cosmic Worldview   120

             Bibliography   128

             Index   132

OUR INALIENABLE LINK TO THE COSMOS

We predict that ten years from now our cosmic origin will be deemed as obvious as the sun being the center of the solar system is considered obvious today. Ask a school child: Where did we come from? Who are we? Where are we heading? The answer without the slightest hesitation will be: We came from space, we are an assembly of cosmic viruses, and ultimately we must return to the cosmos.

With the pace of scientific discoveries in diverse fields from astrophysics to molecular biology that all point in the same direction, a long-overdue paradigm shift from geocentric life to cosmic life appears destined to happen. The result of accepting the new paradigm will be far-reaching and profound.

The oldest human remains—the remains of *Homo sapiens sapiens*—were recently discovered in a cave in Morocco and were dated at about 350,000 years ago. This new discovery pushes back the moment of human origin on Earth more than 100,000 years earlier than was hitherto thought. The theme of this book is that our own genes (DNA), the genes of modern humans, along with the genes of all life on Earth, predated Earth and originated in a vast cosmic context. All our important attributes of life were cosmically fashioned. Instincts for combat, hunting, communication, complex social behavior, and curiosity were all cosmically derived. This deep connection with the universe is one of which we are instinctively aware but so far have chosen to ignore.

The tiniest of viruses, bacteria, microscopic animals (tardigrades), and even seeds of plants have been discovered to be natural space travelers. They can survive in the harsh environment of space and can flit from planet to planet with impunity, building a complex interconnected web of life throughout the cosmos. We humans are effectively part of this web of life; we are no more than complex assemblages of microorganisms, so we owe our links to the wider cosmos. The forces that drive us to ignore this connection will be one of the themes of this book.

The beginnings of our story must go back to the time of Classical Greece. In the fourth century BCE, the Greek philosopher Aristotle, pupil of Plato, tutor to Alexander the Great, made two assertions that were to change the course of history. The first was that Earth was the physical center of the universe, that the stars, planets, and all heavenly bodies revolved around the central Earth. The second was that life of every form arose and continues to arise spontaneously from nonliving inanimate matter on Earth through a mythical process of abiogenesis. Both these assertions turned out to be wrong, but because Aristotle became a towering figure in Western philosophy, his views held sway for centuries.

The first Aristotelean principle, of a geocentric universe, which was held so adamantly and steadfastly, set back the progress of science for many centuries. Only after the completion of the Copernican revolution, which involved the combined efforts of Copernicus, Galileo, Bruno, Tycho Brahe, Kepler, and Newton in the sixteenth, seventeenth, and eighteenth centuries, and after major confrontations with the Catholic Church was the geocentric philosophy finally abandoned. The second Aristotelean principle, of life centered on Earth and arising spontaneously on this planet, continued to dominate philosophy and science for centuries and still continues to do so.

As we shall discuss later there is no doubt that life did not originate on Earth and could not have done so. Nor could it have started de
novo on any one of the hundreds of billions of Earth-like planets that
exist in our Milky Way galaxy alone. From the arguments we advance
in this book we conclude that life, anywhere and everywhere, must
have an ultimate origin that is in some way connected with the beginnings of the universe itself. Every single life-form from the humblest
single-celled organism to the most complex of plants and animals has
an antiquity that stretches as far back in time as we can imagine. Our
inalienable links to the cosmos cannot be ignored. Facts that establish
this viewpoint continue to unfold without remission.

A sonnet by the American poet Edna St. Vincent Millay from her
Collected Sonnets, "Huntsman, What Quarry?," encapsulates the theme
of our book:

> *Upon this gifted age, in its dark hour,*
> *Rains from the sky a meteoric shower*
> *Of facts . . . they lie unquestioned, uncombined.*
> *Wisdom enough to leech us of our ill*
> *Is daily spun; but there exists no loom*
> *To weave it into fabric. . . .*

Our objective in writing this book is to provide the loom to weave
our meteoric shower of facts into fabric. This will be the legacy that our
children and grandchildren will inherit. Will they find the wisdom that
we ourselves were unwilling to accept?

CHAPTER 1

GENESIS OF A THEORY

Orthodoxy means not thinking—not needing to think.
Orthodoxy is unconsciousness.

GEORGE ORWELL, *1984*

This book is about the need for fresh thinking, guided only by facts, and most importantly unfettered by prejudice. Insistence on orthodoxy is the surest recipe for intellectual stagnation. In defense of exploring the heterodox aspects in science, Fred Hoyle once said, "For the big unsolved problems of science it will always be the heterodox solution that turns out to be correct. If the orthodox point of view was correct the relevant problem is solved, so for the most difficult unsolved problems it is the heterodoxy that will always win. The difficulty, however, is to decide which form of heterodoxy is correct."

The heterodoxy that we explore in this book is that we humans are space travelers and so are all other life-forms that inhabit our planet. Every such life-form is a composite assembly of bacteria and viruses that came from space and ultimately arose in a vast cosmic setting. According to this point of view we first arrived on Earth as bacteria and viruses in our cometary spaceships 4.2 billion years ago, as soon as it was cool enough, wet enough, and ready to welcome us and allow us to multiply. Our initial entry was as simple cells (bacterial cells)

4

endowed with the capacity to copy themselves by the process of mito-sis (cell division) and feeding on the organic nutrients that had arrived earlier from space. A single cell thus copies into trillions of similar cells. Most importantly, our next (and still continuing) entry to Earth was as viruses carrying new information, embodying code—genetic code akin to digital computer code—that enters cells and augments their DNA. This is the main process that still continues to drive evolution, leading from simple bacteria to the entire spectrum of life on Earth. In this pic-ture, Darwinian evolution, that is to say, evolution through mutations and natural selection, is relegated to a minor role of optimizing emerg-ing life-forms to their local environments.

The theory of cometary panspermia, the idea that life is a cos-mic phenomenon, was controversial when it was first proposed in the 1970s, but it is now slowly gaining acceptance. On the basis of all the available facts, the theory is vindicated beyond any doubt. But there is

Fig. 1.1. Fred Hoyle talking to Chandra Wickramasinghe in Sri Lanka in 1981

still a residual sociological reluctance to admit that this is so.

When Fred Hoyle (1915–2001) and one of us (CW) first proposed this theory, evidence was, of course, limited compared with what we have today. Our initial starting point was an unexpected astronomical discovery of vast amounts of organic molecules as condensed solid material in interstellar space. The significance of such interstellar organic molecules was scarcely appreciated at the time. But gradually, over the succeeding four decades, they have come to be understood as constituting substantive evidence of our cosmic ancestry. It can no longer be disputed that, at the very least, the complex organic molecules that form the basis of life (and in our view are predominantly the destruction fragments of life) are plentiful in space. But at this point we should stress that such organic molecules that we find in space are a very far cry from the exceedingly complex molecular edifices that we recognize as living cells. The organic molecules that float around in interstellar space can be likened to letters of the alphabet—a, b, c, and so on—and we can imagine them written on the tiles of the word game Scrabble. No matter how vast the number of these letters that are given at random, to go from them to even a single play of Shakespeare would require a miracle of cosmic proportions. That is the magnitude of the information gap to be bridged if we wish to proceed from organic molecules such as the amino acids to all the enzymes that sustain life.

In the 1970s every textbook of biology began with an exposition of the Oparin-Haldane theory of the primordial soup. This was the theory propounded in the 1920s independently by British scientist J. B. S. Haldane and Russian biochemist Aleksandr Oparin. This was an Earth-centered theory based on the Aristotelean idea of the spontaneous generation of life. According to Aristotle, life arises spontaneously from inanimate matter on Earth whenever and wherever appropriate conditions prevailed. He gives us many examples, one of which is his statement that fireflies emerge from a mixture of warm earth and morning

Fig. 1.2. Aristotle

dew. Aristotle acquired the reputation of being a meticulous observer of all aspects of the world around him, but upon close scrutiny many of his observations, although philosophically elegant and even poetic, were actually found to be false.

Aristotle's writings include discourses on politics, ethics, philosophy, and mathematics, as well as astronomy and biology. Some of his flawed scientific ideas were carried through for many centuries for the simple reason that Aristotle remained a revered and influential figure from antiquity to modern times.

Ironically, the progress of Western science in the post-Renaissance era often began with a confrontation with the fallacious ideas of Aristotle—for instance, his concept of an Earth-centered universe. Today we accept that Earth is an insignificant planet orbiting an ordinary star (the sun) in our Milky Way galaxy. We know from recent studies that there are well over a hundred billion planets more or less like Earth in the Milky Way alone, and there are countless galaxies similar to the Milky Way throughout the observable universe. So there is no longer any resistance to downgrading the status of our home planet, Earth, to that of a mere "speck of dust" in the cosmic context. The situation has been different, however, in relation to the origins of life.

While it took approximately two thousand years for Aristotle's geocentric view of the universe to be overturned, his theory of the spontaneous generation of life would continue to be upheld by the scientific community for centuries to follow. The primordial soup theory developed by Haldane and Oparin in the 1920s, which became mainstream, was inspired by Aristotle's ideas. Experiments carried out three decades later, in the 1950s, by Harold Urey and Stanley Miller showed how organic molecules (the simple "alphabet" molecules of life) could be formed relatively easily from inorganic chemicals such as water, methane, and ammonia in the atmosphere.

Today no one doubts that such simple organic molecules may have formed in the early Earth's atmosphere in the manner demonstrated by

Urey and Miller, or they may even have been added from space, raining down into the oceans to form a primordial soup of organic molecules. But the relevance of all this to the origin of life remains highly questionable. Organic molecules—amino acids and nucleotides among others—as we have mentioned, are a very far cry from life. Life even in its humblest form is superastronomically complex, far too complex to arise from random shuffling of molecules in a pond, an ocean, or even a hydrothermal vent.

The mind-blowing complexity of living systems lies in the highly specific arrangements of molecules—amino acids in enzyme chains or nucleotides in DNA or RNA. The required arrangements for a functioning cell cannot be arrived at by the random shuffling of component molecules. A metaphor that has been used to illustrate this problem is not an exaggeration in any sense. We have said that a random origin of life from organic molecules is like a tornado blowing through a junkyard and then assembling a Boeing 747. We must regard the origin of life as being so exceedingly improbable that it has to be considered as a one-off, a unique cosmological event. Once it has originated its incorporation in interstellar dust and comets, its indefinite persistence throughout the universe would follow. All these processes have been discussed in detail elsewhere (e.g. Wickramasinghe 2015; Steele et al. 2018).

A satisfactory theory must not only explain an existing body of facts, but it must also be able to make testable predictions. This latter requirement was fully met for the theory of cosmic life. After our proposal of cosmic life was made in 1981, new techniques and experimental developments led to the generation of new and often unexpected facts. Testing predictions of the theory against a rapidly growing body of facts then became a priority.

If viruses and bacteria of cosmic origin were to be transferred across astronomical and cosmological distances, a continual existence of such material should be observed in interstellar space. With organic molecules

Fig. 1.3. The Horsehead Nebula is a cloud of biological dust in the Milky Way that is dense enough to block the light from background stars. (Image courtesy of NASA)

already discovered in interstellar space, it did not take much effort to propose explicit tests for the presence of bacteria, viruses, and their breakup products in interstellar clouds. The test was to compare the absorption characteristics of cosmic dust and the laboratory properties of bacteria under the conditions they would encounter in interstellar space. If our theory is valid these two spectra (data sets) should coincide.

Our first prediction of the theory of cosmic life was thus fulfilled with amazing precision. As expected our critics were not pleased! Their response was to say, "This is no surprise; a bacterium is made of many simpler chemical structures, and if you mix such structures in the correct proportions the bacterial spectrum would be reproduced." Strictly true, but hardly probable. This was a case of reviving the epicycles of Ptolemy, which were invented to avoid the conclusion that the sun was the center of our planetary system.

The next key development, which took place in 1986, was concerned with the return of Halley's Comet after seventy-six years. This was, in fact, the first comet that came under close scrutiny after the dawn of the space age. The popular view at the time was that comets were dirty snowballs (Fred Lawrence Whipple's "dirty snowball" cometary hypothesis), which came to be demolished fairly quickly by observations that were made in April 1986 using satellites as well as ground-based telescopes.

Before the actual rendezvous of the Giotto space probe with Halley's Comet in April 1986, nobody had ever seen the nucleus of a comet—only their spectacular tails had been seen and photographed—and people had to theorize and conjecture as to the existence and the nature of the comet's nucleus or core. Ahead of the observations of 1986 being made, Fred Hoyle and one of us (CW) made a firm prediction, based on our organic comet model, that when a comet was heated in sunlight near its perihelion (closest approach to the sun), it would boil off bacterial dust and turn into a black coal-like body. This prediction was dramatically verified. Moreover, an infrared spectrum of the comet's dust tail was found to match the spectrum of a bacterium to an amazing degree of precision.

Since 1986, a wealth of data, gleaned from ground-based telescopes as well as space probes, has accumulated relating to other comets. In no instance could we find any contradiction with our biological model of comet dust, although astronomers are still loath to admit this fact.

*Fig. 1.4. Halley's Comet (1986) from the ground (top) and Comet 67P/C-G
from the* Rosetta *space probe (2015) (Images courtesy of NASA)*

The latest example, the *Rosetta* space probe's examination of the comet 67P/C-G has generated a wealth of data that can only be explained satisfactorily and rationally on the basis of a biological model of the dust. Yet there appears to be a concerted effort on the part of a majority of scientists and science journalists to say that although life-related organic molecules have been found in large quantities in comets, they cannot or need not signify life.

A resistance to accept that life exists in vast quantities in comets and elsewhere in the universe appears deep-rooted in the human psyche. Perhaps this is a natural extension of the earlier resistance to departing from the Aristotelean viewpoint that our planet was the center of the solar system and hence also of the universe. It may also be part and parcel of human psychology to believe that we are unique and all-important. For egocentrism is a necessary by-product of the geocentric viewpoint that we had cherished for so long.

Life on our planet Earth retains a hallowed and sacred status today. By asserting that life emerged de novo on Earth and thereafter evolved in a "closed box" environment through processes entirely confined to Earth, we instantly exclude any possible biological influence from the external universe. This position is turning out to be fundamentally flawed, and the sooner we realize it and discard it the better.

Ongoing advances in microbiology, including the discovery that many types of microbes can withstand the harshest imaginable environments, both on Earth and in space, all point to their cosmic origin. Microorganisms have been recovered from the abdomens of insects that were trapped and fossilized in amber for over thirty million years. In a recent study a deep frozen lake in Antarctica, sealed away from the outside world for over fifteen million years, has yielded DNA evidence of life, including complex life, persisting under four kilometers of frozen ice. Recently it has been reported that two algal species placed on the exterior of the International Space Station survived for sixteen months, enduring extreme temperature fluctuations and the vacuum of space, as well as considerable UV and cosmic radiation. Seeds of flowering plants have also been shown to survive and germinate after exposure to space conditions.

Even more astonishing are the survival properties of tardigrades (water bears), which are millimeter-sized animals that can survive desiccation, extremely high and low temperatures, the highest imaginable doses of ionizing radiation, and the vacuum of space. There is no Darwinian sense whatsoever by which any of these extreme survival attributes could have evolved in isolation on Earth. Only in the context of an open cosmic system, with an imperative for surviving space travel, could any of these properties be understood.

Another aspect of the theory of cosmic life that surfaced quite early was a connection with disease, a connection that was also linked to evolution. In diverse cultures throughout the world comets were feared as well as worshipped. They were regarded as bringers of life and also of pestilence, disease, and death. One might well wonder whether these ancient beliefs had a direct basis in facts that were meticulously observed and recorded without prejudice. We tend to dismiss all such ancient beliefs as being ignorant superstitions. This may not be true. Would it not be surprising if the people of all the great civilizations—Egyptians, Chinese, and Indians—were ignorant or stupid in this regard? Rather, it is likely that they respected facts for what they were, much more than contemporary societies that are too often constrained by prejudice. It is with such considerations in mind that Fred Hoyle and one of us (CW) began to reexamine all the available data—historic and modern—of pandemics of disease.

We soon discovered that devastating plagues in history swept across vast tracts of land, descending it would seem from nowhere. Often they came suddenly and disappeared equally suddenly. In 430 BCE, a devastating plague struck the city of Athens, which was then under siege by Sparta during the Peloponnesian War (431–404 BCE). In the next three years, most of the population was infected, and perhaps as many as a quarter of the city's population died. The historian Thucydides left an eyewitness account of this plague, giving a detailed description of its symptoms. Modern physicians who examined these facts have not succeeded in identifying the disease as any known plague. A hitherto unknown disease caused by a pathogenic virus or bacterium of space origin seems to have been involved in 430 BCE.

The Plague of Justinian (541–542 CE) struck Europe in the sixth century and is estimated to have killed between thirty and fifty million people—about half the world's population at that time. About eight hundred years later the Black Death struck, killing fifty million people between 1347 and 1351. It has recently been suggested that both plagues were spread to humans by rats whose fleas carried the bacteria, but where the bacteria came from in the first instance remains a puzzle.

Careful examination of a vast body of data led Fred Hoyle and one of us (CW) to conclude in 1979 that pathogenic bacteria and viruses delivered to Earth from comets provided the best explanation for many pandemics in history (Hoyle and Wickramasinghe 1979). Of particular interest to us was the study of influenza, and especially the Spanish flu pandemic of 1918 and 1919, which caused some thirty million deaths worldwide. Reviewing all the available data on this pandemic, Dr. Louis Weinstein wrote thus in the *New England Journal of Medicine* of May 6, 1976:

> The influenza pandemic of 1918 occurred in three waves. The first appeared in the winter and spring of 1917–1918. . . . The lethal second wave, which started at Fort Devens in Ayer, Massachusetts, on September 12, 1918, involved almost the entire world over a very short time. . . . Its epidemiological behavior was most unusual. Although person-to-person spread occurred in local areas, the disease appeared on the same day in widely separated parts of the world on the one hand, but, on the other, took days to weeks to spread

relatively short distances. It was detected in Boston and Bombay on the same day, but took three weeks before it reached New York City, despite the fact that there was considerable travel between the two cities. It was present for the first time at Joliet in the State of Illinois four weeks after it was detected in Chicago, the distance between those areas being only 38 miles. (Weinstein 1976)

With no long-distance air travel in 1918, simultaneous first strikes in Boston and Bombay offer in our view strong evidence of a component of the virus falling in from space.

All this goes to confirm that spaceborne viruses not only cause disease but also play a crucial role in the evolution of life. On February 12, 2001, the code for the entire human genome was deciphered. A multitude of ancient viral footprints have been discovered in the genomes of all multicelled life-forms. It also came as a surprise that a large fraction of our DNA, perhaps as high as 5 percent, is in some way connected with viral sequences. And a subset of this is in the form of what we now recognize to be related to species-specific "retroviruses," of a type of which the AIDS virus is just one example. Our own ancestral line—which led through primates and anthropoids to *Homo sapiens* over hundreds of millions of years—shows clearly the relics of repeated viral or retroviral attacks presumably similar to AIDS. At each such viral attack the evolving line was almost completely culled, leaving only a small surviving and immune breeding group to carry through with a relic form of this virus tucked away in its genome.

Viral sequences thus added through the mechanism of disease provide evolutionary potential that could lead to new genotypes and new species at one end of the scale and to new traits and the capacity to express our genes in novel ways at the other. It is becoming clear that our entire existence on this planet is contingent on the continuing ingress of cosmic viruses, which we had hitherto thought were merely the vehicles for disastrous pandemics of disease. Their positive role in evolution, which was predicted by Hoyle and one of us (Hoyle and Wickramasinghe 1982) is only just beginning to be revealed. The benefits that would follow from such a realization and acceptance can scarcely be imagined at the present time.

CHAPTER 2

THE DEEPEST QUESTIONS

Into this Universe, and why not knowing,
Nor whence, like Water willy-nilly flowing!
And out of it, as Wind along the Waste,
I know not whither, willy-nilly blowing.

THE RUBAIYAT OF OMAR KHAYAM (STANZA 29),

TRANSLATED BY EDWARD FITZGERALD

Where have we come from? Where are we going? What are we here for? Is life unique to this rocky planet we call Earth? These are the deepest of philosophical questions and perhaps the very first that were asked as soon as *Homo sapiens* acquired the intellectual capacity to do so. The first answers, as far as we can glean from surviving fragmentary evidence—folklore and cave art—invariably turned to the skies. The spectacle of the Milky Way must surely have overwhelmed our ancestors, as, indeed, it overwhelms us today. This sense of awe may have led directly to the concept of the sun god and other gods, all of whom were placed in the skies. The humans—*Homo sapiens*—were still helpless creatures beholden and subservient to the inexorable power of the universe. The harsh vicissitudes of nature—droughts, floods, storms at sea, earthquakes—all contributed to enslave and humiliate them. They needed the gods of the heavens to provide psychological comfort, solace, and safe passage through the journey of life.

Humankind's subservience to nature has found expression in art from the earliest cave paintings to modern times. Paul Gauguin's 1897 painting with the title *Where Do We Come From? What Are We? Where Are We Going?* says it all. These are the same questions we continue to ask even in the present day.

With advances in technology some of the cruelest forces of nature were tamed. Civilization marched forward, and our ancestors began to feel they were more and more in control of their destiny. Control appeared to shift from the universe, with its capricious ever-changing patterns, to the fixed Earth, which was deemed constant, eternal, and largely under human control.

We realize now, or at least we should have realized, that our entire genetic heritage (except for minor tweaking) came from the vast external universe. Earth was just an insignificant building site on which the blueprint of all life came to be assembled into a great multitude of different forms. Throughout the universe there are countless other building sites, more or less like Earth, on which the same process must have occurred. So the humbling realization is that we humans, and indeed all other life on Earth, are utterly unimportant in the wider cosmic context.

One of the most exciting areas of modern astronomy is the search for planets orbiting distant stars—planets that are habitable and more or less similar to Earth. As we have noted earlier, many studies directed at such searches are presently underway, deploying telescopes that are in orbit around Earth. The currently estimated tally of Earth-like planets runs to over a hundred billion in our galaxy alone—averaging about one "Earth" for every sunlike star. The implication is that the average separation between two Earth-like planets is a mere four light years. This incredibly short distance in cosmic terms clearly implies that exchanges of bacteria and viruses between such planets are not only *possible,*

Fig. 2.1. Artist's depictions of the planet around our nearest star, Proxima Centauri. Adapted from original material from the European Space Agency. (Images courtesy of ESA)

but *inevitable.* Very recently astronomers have detected evidence for a rocky planet like Earth orbiting our nearest neighboring star, Proxima Centauri. This star is only 3.1 light years away from Earth—a spitting distance in cosmic terms. Living material in the form of bacteria and viruses that reached Earth over the past four billion years must surely have reached the planet around Proxima Centauri as well. Life very similar to Earth life may well have flourished there, built from cosmic genetic building blocks.

Evidence for the most ancient bacterial life on Earth has recently been discovered in the form of carbon globules trapped within crystals of the mineral zircon and deposited in rocks that formed 4.1 to 4.2 billion years ago during the so-called Hadean epoch. At that time Earth was being relentlessly bombarded by comets, the same comets that also brought water to form Earth's oceans. It is reasonable to infer that the same impacting comets also delivered the first life to our planet in the form of bacteria and viruses. Thereafter the addition of viruses from comets expanded the genomes of evolving life on Earth in the manner we have already discussed. One dramatic event 540 million years ago, the Cambrian explosion of multicelled life, is now known to have brought essentially all the genes that were needed to generate the entire range of evolutionary development witnessed in the record of life on Earth.

We have noted earlier that the information content of life at the molecular level is of a superastronomical magnitude. The logical conclusion is that this crucial information for life's origin and evolution is always present in the universe and that genes carrying such information are continually amplified and distributed through the agency of comets. Bacterial and viral genes delivered to Earth are continually being added to genomes of evolving life-forms. Major evolutionary traits in the development of complex life are all externally derived, and evolution itself is a process that is essentially driven from outside. If this is the case, the

Fig. 2.2. Comets impacting Earth both bring new life and take existing life away. Some sixty-five million years ago, an impacting comet caused the extinction of the dinosaurs and nearly 85 percent of all life on Earth. (Image courtesy of NASA)

overall impression will be of a preprogramming leading to the higher levels of development in biology. The evolution of the eye may be cited as one example of this type. Even some less definable manifestations of gene expression in our own hominid line of descent, for example, the emergence of genes for higher levels of cognition, bear the signs of "preprogramming" or pre-evolution.

We now know that impacts of asteroids and comets on planets laden with life can not only cause extinctions of species (e.g., the extinction of the dinosaurs on Earth sixty-five million years ago) but can also splash back into space life-laden material (dust and meteorites) that can reach neighboring planets. We can argue that Darwinian-style evolution occurred not on any one planet such as Earth but was spread over innumerable habitats in the grandest possible cosmic setting. Whatever happened, it is clear that life cannot be regarded as unique or confined to Earth. Life on Earth implies life everywhere. The entire galaxy, our Milky Way system, can therefore be regarded as one single gigantic connected biosphere. It follows that life of all the types and forms known on Earth, ranging from bacteria to plants, animals, and even intelligent life, must, to a high degree of probability, be all-pervasive. This is now not just a theory but an inescapable fact.

If a single discovery is to serve as a watershed in the journey to proving our cosmic origins, it is a recent study of two related species: the squid and the octopus (Steele et al. 2018). The squid has an antiquity in the geological record that goes back to the great metazoan explosion of multicelled life-forms 540 million years ago. The octopus apparently branches out from the squid line about 400 million years ago, presumed to have evolved from an ancestral squid. Recent DNA sequencing of the squid and octopus genomes has exploded a bombshell. The squid contains a very meager complement of genes adequate to serve its modest survival needs. The emergent octopus, on the other hand, has over 40,000 genes (we the humans have only 25,000 genes), and many of these genes code for complex brain function. Others code for a highly sophisticated camouflage capability, including rapid switches of color. The octopus is incredibly more complex in structure and performance than its squid predecessor. Where did the suite of genes coding for complex brain function come from? They were not present in the ancestral squid or in any other living form that existed on Earth at the time. The clear implication is that they came from outside Earth—external to terrestrial biology, part of the cosmic heritage of life.

The million-dollar questions that remain: Who or what could have put all this together? What kind of agent or agencies conceived this grand scheme of things? One thing is beyond dispute: Life in its totality is the most complex informational system imaginable. How the information of life was put together remains one of the great unsolved mysteries of science, one that touches on cosmological ideas as well as religious beliefs.

The Aristotelean view that life started on Earth spontaneously in the primordial soup implicitly invokes a deus ex machina, essentially a miracle or an act of God. This is, of course, not openly admitted in our modern scientific culture, a culture that is turning increasingly to the rejection of God and to atheism as an intellectual choice. In our view the obstinate insistence of an Earth-based origin of life is a clear indication of a religious and cultural preference that dominates today, particularly in the Western world. The same preference holds also when it comes to the origin of the universe itself; the standard form of big bang cosmology is uncannily similar to a scientific rendering of the first page of Genesis. We shall return to this in chapter 12.

The clear implication of the ideas we discussed is that the essential blueprint for all life, the information for every gene in every life-form that could ever arise, is always present in the form of viruses and viral genes and distributed over a vast cosmological volume. It is possible that life at its genetic level *never* arose as such but was *always* present in an eternal and unchanging cosmos. This point of view is more in consonance with Eastern philosophies that predate Greek as well as Judeo-Christian ideas by millennia.

CHAPTER 3

A COSMIC CREATOR?

Then to the rolling Heav'n itself I cried,
Asking, "What Lamp had Destiny to guide
Her little Children stumbling in the Dark?
And—"A blind Understanding!" Heav'n replied.

THE RUBAIYAT OF OMAR KHAYAM (STANZA 33),

TRANSLATED BY EDWARD FITZGERALD

Omar Khayam (1048–1131 CE) was a great Persian poet, astronomer, and mathematician. As a mathematician he is most famous for devising geometrical solutions of cubic equations, and his astronomical work included the construction of a calendar that remained the most accurate computation of time for many centuries. His work as a poet came to be discovered and recognized only much later, particularly with the discovery and translation by Edward Fitzgerald of the *Rubaiyat*—a long poem consisting of some seventy quatrains expressing religious and philosophical skepticism and a hedonistic attitude to life.

In the modern world hedonism, in which the pursuit of pleasure is considered the greatest good, still prevails, but the most divisive factor in the conduct of human affairs has turned out to be religion. Religious differences, no matter how small, have the potential to lead to bitter strife. The ongoing disputes in the Middle East between Christians, Jews, and Muslims have deep historical roots. Among Muslims themselves the differences between Sunnis, Shiites, and members of other sects can spark bitter conflict with the slightest provocation. When we realize and accept our inalienable cosmic origins, such religious conflicts may perhaps be expected to abate. We would begin to understand that all religions represent but imperfect attempts to interpret our cosmic origins and to assign a cosmic purpose for our existence. The differences between Eastern and Western religions in this regard and their impact on science will be the subject of chapter 8.

As we have already mentioned, the deepest mystery of life is concealed in a simple biochemical fact: the grotesque improbability of abiogenesis—turning nonliving matter to life. Life anywhere starting

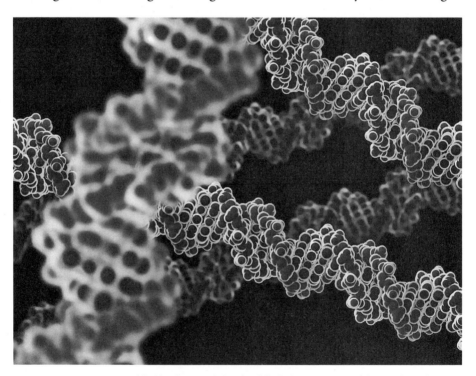

Fig. 3.1. To assemble the bases of the double helix in DNA (the nucleotides adenine, thymine, cytosine, and guanine) in the correct order to carry out the functions of a cell essentially involves a "miracle."

spontaneously from the coming together of basic chemicals—amino acids to make enzymes or nucleotides to make DNA and RNA—is utterly and hopelessly improbable.

Alongside the specific complexity of the enzymes and DNA, we must also take account of the "program" needed to control the behavior of a living cell. This itself requires a degree of logical complexity that is beyond comprehension at the present time. Anyone who has set up a sophisticated code for a computer will know that by far the most difficult part lies in devising the logic of the main program, not in the subroutines. In the biological case, the enzymes, DNA, and so forth are only the subroutines. The main program, which still remains obscure, is probably much less likely to be discovered by random processes than even the individual enzymes.

If a modern biochemist were given a complete listing of the amino acid sequences of all the five hundred enzymes in the simplest bacterium, *Mycoplasma genitalium,* he or she could construct the sequences with complete accuracy, hence demonstrating the enormous superiority of intelligence over blind random processes. Given sufficient effort and dedication to the task, all the complex biopolymers in a living cell could be constructed from their component molecules, and if the grand master program of the cell were known, it is quite likely that it too could be constructed in the same way. In short, it is not beyond human capacity—perhaps realizable within the next hundred years—to make a fully functioning living cell. This will, of course, demand as a prerequisite that we are given the blueprint (DNA sequence) as well as the biotechnological know-how to proceed.

This immediately raises the question of whether life as we know it can possibly be the product of intelligent design. This is a logical possibility, of course, but it has become very unfashionable in recent years because the idea of intelligent design has been incorrectly equated to a particular religious doctrine—Christian fundamentalism. Be that as it may, the purely logical case for an intelligent design operating to start life is beyond reproach. The intelligent designer in question would have to be superintelligent, of course, perhaps many orders of magnitude more advanced technologically than modern humans in 2019. Judging from the present exponential rate of progress of technology of all kinds, this possibility cannot be ruled out by logic alone.

But the question next arises: What would be the point of going to such trouble if the information for life already existed in the functioning of the superintelligent life-form itself? Even if we could show that the assembly was for some specified purpose, we would be no further along in our progress in understanding our origins. We would still have to explain how the enzymes came to be assembled in the first place in order to permit our ancestral *Homo sapiens* to emerge and our postulated cosmic superintelligence to eventually emerge.

To be logically consistent we must assert that the intelligence that put together the enzymes, DNA, and so forth in the first place was of "another" totally alien form and did not itself contain these particular information-rich, carbon-based molecules. The hypothetical intelligence belonged to a *different* life-form with a totally distinct chemistry. Perhaps we can argue that carbon-based life was, in fact, invented by a non-carbon-based living form that had achieved a very much higher level of intelligence.

Silicon is an atom, also synthesized in stars, bearing some similarity to carbon, and there has often been speculation as to whether a life-form based on silicon instead of carbon might exist. This has been the stuff of science fiction and Hollywood blockbusters so far. Yet if one attempts to follow a chemical system similar to that which operates in our carbon-based life for the element silicon—silicon sugars, silicon nucleic acids, silicon proteins, and so on—the idea soon grinds to a halt, because it is easy to show that, although generally similar, silicon is far less versatile chemically than carbon. So we might conclude that a siliceous form of life is exceedingly unlikely to have preceded the carbonaceous form, if the two are thought of in terms of similar chemistries.

But what if we forget about chemistry in the way that our form of carbon-based life functions and focus attention on electronics or robotics? Then it will surely be the element silicon that wins handsomely over carbon. We all know of the silicon chip in our smartphones, tablets, and computers, but nobody considers the possibility of a carbon chip. That would be an electronic absurdity unless some unknown property of low-temperature carbon remains still to be discovered. Leaving that

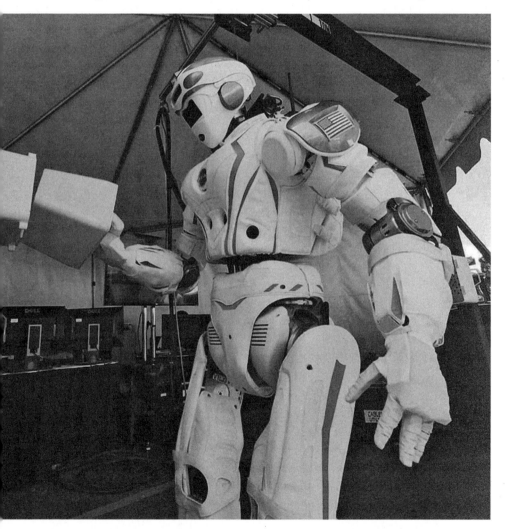

Fig. 3.2. A humanoid robot constructed by NASA to perform routine jobs.
(Image courtesy of NASA)

aside, we might assume, as a working hypothesis, that our progenitor life-form was in essence an extremely complex silicon chip.

As stated earlier, it would not be possible for an intelligence, no matter how great, to devise and create carbonaceous life without performing an immense amount of digital number crunching— working out a superastronomical number of options for enzymes at least! The best way we know to perform the necessary calculations would be through deploying the silicon chip in a large battery of supercomputers.

If this is the way it happened, we would have the logical sequence (in which the arrows mean "leading to"):

silicon chip life-form → carbonaceous life → silicon chip life-form

By such a logical progression, including the conscious intervention of our "created" carbon-based life-form, the silicon chip life-form would succeed in spreading itself unstoppably. With our present-day interest in robots, robots being endowed with silicon chips, the above logic may be replaced more explicitly by:

robots → carbonaceous life → robots

Since robots cannot be conceived of as self-propagators, carbonaceous life can be seen as the essential intermediary step to disseminate silicon-based robotic life on the widest possible scale throughout the universe. This is our raison d'être, the purpose for the invention of carbonaceous life. All this is conceivable within our present state of scientific and technological knowledge with perhaps only a minimal amount of extrapolation. Yet if this were all there is, there would still be a lack of grandeur in our scheme of things. To proceed further to higher levels of abstraction, we can write:

?? → silicon chip robot → carbonaceous life → silicon chip robot

Our subservience now is to some undefined God-like entity, noted here as ?? It is more "respectable" in our eyes than a silicon chip robot, if only for the reason that it is not defined.

Let us now turn to possible candidates for the entity denoted by ?? Remarkably, we perhaps have some evidence to guide us. Life—our type of carbon-based life—depends on oxygen and carbon being roughly equal in their cosmic abundances. If either one dominated markedly over the other, carbon-based life would not be possible. The requirement is for oxygen to be rather more abundant than carbon, which is exactly how things actually stand in the universe.

As Fred Hoyle showed in the 1950s, both of these elements— carbon and oxygen—are produced from helium in nuclear reactions that occur in the deep interiors of stars similar to the sun. It is precisely this process of nuclear burning that keeps the sun shining and makes possible the existence of life on Earth. This process—producing carbon and oxygen and other elements in stellar nuclear furnaces—operates not only for the sun but also for hundreds of billions of similar stars in our Milky Way galaxy and beyond.

So, far from the relative abundances of carbon and oxygen coming out correctly in an unavoidable way, it turns out that getting conditions right depends on a couple of remarkable properties and coincidences. One is a property of the carbon nucleus, the other of the oxygen nucleus. (Both the 7.65 MeV [million electron volts] level of the carbon nucleus and the 7.12 MeV level of the oxygen nucleus must be tuned very closely to these particular energy values.)

The level of intelligence or perhaps superintelligence needed to control the properties of the oxygen and carbon nuclei would be exceedingly high. The superintelligence would do so by controlling what are called the coupling constants of physics. These are arbitrary numbers that appear in physics empirically—numbers that could in theory have any value, but we determine them by experiment. They can be obtained only by reference to the real world rather than from logical argument. The basic unit of electrical charge (the charge of the electron) is one such number. So far as the constancy of physics is concerned, the unit of an electrical charge could apparently have an infinite number of values other than the value we assign to it from observation and experiment.

The coupling constants determine the favorable aspects of physics, like the desired properties of the carbon and oxygen nuclei. It would be by controlling the values of the coupling constants that a supreme intelligence might determine a wide range of features of the universe. These include the strengths of the forces of gravity and the attractive force between electrons and protons. Such properties affect in turn how stars and planets that could harbor life can form from interstellar gas clouds. The remarkable chemical behavior of the carbon atom and the electronic properties of the silicon chip are other crucial examples of properties that might also be controlled or manipulated in such a way.

We have now moved on to an altogether higher level of intelligence than the silicon chip. Calculating the properties of the enzymes would surely be an amazing achievement, judged from the human level, but likely enough it would seem rather a simple matter to an intelligence that could control the coupling constants of physics so that the universe can even exist in the first place. It is against this backdrop that we can now propose the identity of our superintelligence:

> Control over the coupling constants of physics = ??
> The temptation next is to postulate that ?? = God.

We thereby terminate the chain of logic. But such a conclusion leads to further problems. It leaves the relationship of God to the universe unresolved. The enigmatic entity (??) would still be only a part of the universe, *within* the universe, and therefore God would only be a part of the universe. This can be regarded as an unsatisfactory conclusion. A more satisfactory solution might be to posit an infinite sequence of entities:

$$\ldots ????? \rightarrow ???? \rightarrow ??? \rightarrow ?? \rightarrow$$

silicon chip robot → carbonaceous life → silicon chip robot

Where does the sequence going to the left stop? It doesn't. It goes on and on and on, with ever-rising levels of intelligence denoted by more and more question marks. But like a convergent mathematical sequence of functions, it tends to an idealized limit, so that by going far enough to the left the terms differ by as little as one pleases from the idealized limit. It is this idealized "mathematical" limit that is God, and it is the universe itself, as Sir James Jeans had asserted in his *Mysterious Universe* many decades ago:

God = universe

And the logical system is now closed.

CHAPTER 4

THE NATURE OF CONSCIOUSNESS

Dream's evanescence, the way in which, on awakening,
our thoughts thrust it aside as something bizarre, and
our reminiscences mutilating or rejecting it—all these
and many other problems have for many hundred years
demanded answers which up till now could never have
been satisfactory.

SIGMUND FREUD, *THE INTERPRETATION OF DREAMS*

We all think we know what it means to be conscious. Consciousness can be interpreted at many different levels. It is an essential part of being human; arguably it may also be an entity common to nonhuman life, not only on Earth but everywhere in the universe. It may even be a property intrinsic to the universe itself that we are still a long way from comprehending. The medical description of consciousness is more restricted, being defined as the state of being awake, aware, and responsive to pain; unconsciousness would be the opposite.

Concepts akin to consciousness have an ancient pedigree. They can be traced back to ritual, mysticism, and a variety of mystical cults in the ancient world. These cults, often with their elaborate rituals of dance

34

and song, sought to deal with the most intractable problems associated with the human condition. The Pythagoreans were one such ancient cult, which was supposedly led by the great mathematician Pythagoras; they believed in the transmutation of souls, rebirth, and the existence of an underworld, all linked directly or indirectly to notions of consciousness. The Greek philosopher Plato (fifth century BCE) argued for the immortality of the soul in his dialogue *Phaedo*. He believed in reincarnation as an eternal cyclic process and postulated a sharp distinction between the mortal body and the soul. A soul that survives organic death in most ancient traditions could be identified with a return of consciousness to some eternal cosmic reservoir.

The Socratic views on consciousness, based on the teachings of the Greek philosopher Socrates (470–399 BCE), are remarkably similar to very much older ideas that prevailed in ancient India. These ideas were set out in the form of verses exploring a wide range of matters relating to the human condition and to the cosmos at large. It is thought that they were composed around the period from 1700 to 1100 BCE, probably by many authors, and preserved as an oral tradition until they were written down around 300 BCE. According to the Vedas (the main text being the Rig Veda [see figure 4.1 on page 36]), the self (human consciousness) and the cosmos are inextricably intertwined. Self is in this sense a manifestation of the cosmos. Every single particle, every living being is an expression of a cosmic consciousness that is posited to be eternal and all pervasive. If the universe really began with a big bang and if life started within it, what preceded it was cosmic consciousness. This may well be the ????? to the left of the relationship we discussed in the last chapter:

(A) ????? = Cosmic consciousness → universe

From the time of Euclid we became familiar with a world in which there are three dimensions—length, breadth, and height. For nearly a century now we have also come to be familiar with the fourth dimension—

time. Einstein's relativistic universe requires a "four dimensional space-time continuum" in order to account for all the known facts relating to the physics of atoms on the one hand and to the universe of planets, stars, and galaxies on the other. According to Einstein's theory, astronomically large

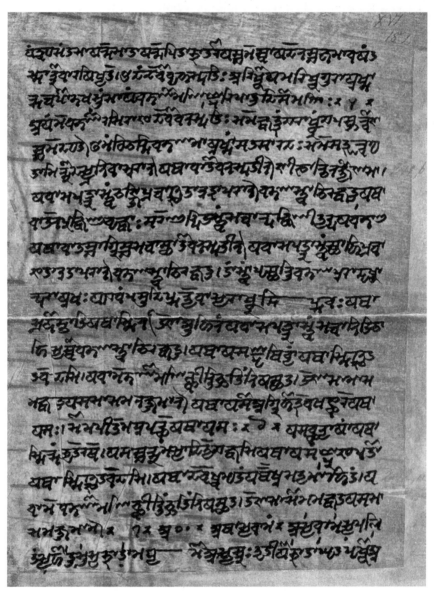

Fig. 4.1. A page of the Rig Veda
(set in written form at around 300 BCE)

masses—planets, stars, galaxies—cause the curvature in space-time, and this phenomenon connects gravity with space and time.

It is fashionable nowadays to consider spaces of higher dimension—five, six, seven, and even higher dimensions—particularly in relation to subatomic particles and the theory known as string theory in physics. Could consciousness and our very existence as sentient beings be somehow connected with such higher dimensions? Could the question marks in equation (A) on page 35 straddle a multiplicity of hitherto unchartered dimensions of the real world?

Nobel laureate Eugene Wigner (1902–1995) first developed the idea that quantum mechanics is somehow connected with consciousness, in particular with human consciousness. Following the pioneering work in quantum physics of Erwin Schrödinger (1887–1961) and his wave function description of the quantum world, a puzzle emerged that led Wigner and others to suggest this connection. Schrödinger's wave equation describes a "state" of a quantum system in terms of probabilities. An electron in an atom, for instance, can be in one of several states, say A, B, C . . . , and which state it actually occupies is given in terms of a probability. Classical ideas of determinism are thrown away in the context of the quantum subatomic world. The probabilities of A, B, C, and so forth can be calculated precisely by solving Schrödinger's so-called wave equation. However, the human observer who makes a measurement of the system at any moment finds it to be in just one of these several states—say state A. The active intervention of the conscious observer would appear to play a crucial role in turning a *probable* outcome predicted by quantum theory into a unique and *definite* result.

Schrödinger devised a famous thought experiment to illustrate this problem:

A cat was placed in a box containing a vial of lethal poison and a quantity of a radioactive atom. The arrangement ensured that the poison was released when the radioactive atom decayed. Since radioactive decay is a probabilistic process, there is, say, a 50/50 chance that the cat is dead or alive when the lid of the box is opened by an inquisitive observer. Would a random observer find the cat dead or alive? The answer is that the cat will be found both dead and alive on the basis of theory. But, of course, an actual observer who opens the lid would see just one of the two possible results. Schrödinger thus argued that the conscious observer essentially caused the collapse of the uncertainty, "the collapse of the quantum mechanical wave function" as it is called.

We next explore the question of where in our bodies does consciousness reside? Is it inside us, within the brain, or is it a property or manifestation of the external universe with which we somehow interact? For more than half a century, scientists have attempted to explain consciousness and the mind on the basis of electrochemical processes in the brain involving a class of cells known as neurons. Such attempts have largely failed. There is a growing body of evidence, however, to support the idea that a nonmaterial "mind" and a physical brain involving neurons are separate entities engaged in a mutual communicating relationship. It is this relationship that manifests itself in consciousness.

In the latter part of the nineteenth century, when scientists came to recognize the existence of consciousness as a phenomenon in its own right, it was hoped that experimental psychology and brain anatomy would quickly unveil its true nature. That was not to be. For several decades the sciences of neurophysiology and psychology have tried to explore the workings of the human brain *without* bringing in mind or consciousness as extrinsic entities, but they have mostly failed.

The real hope to unravel the secrets of consciousness began to emerge when the workings of the brain came to be analyzed at a deeper quantum level. Roger Penrose and Stuart Hameroff developed a theory that collections of microtubules within neurons could act coherently as some kind of quantum computer and serve essentially as "instruments" capable of generating consciousness and communicating with the external world. Penrose has described physical mechanisms involved in consciousness as lying in the gray area of physics that straddles classical and quantum mechanics.

The brain-computer analogy has been discussed over a few decades, but it gives only an incomplete picture of what may be going on. Modern computers carry out computations at lightning speed, and they can make millions of "decisions" within prescribed limits and rules. They can play chess and perhaps even beat a grand master. But a computer can still not be deemed conscious or intelligent, and it acts only within the laws of classical deterministic physics. It could make random errors rarely, but it could not come up with flashes of intuition revealing new relationships within the universe. The same limitation applies to the rapidly growing field of artificial intelligence and robotics. The supercomputer or the intelligent robot can do marvelous things, but they are able to do these things only because there is an intelligent human operator somewhere in control making deliberate conscious decisions.

The emerging trend of contemporary science is in the direction of admitting, albeit reluctantly, the existence of an essentially nonorganic, nonmaterial superstructure connected to the brain and identifiable as a "conscious mind." If that is acknowledged as a fact, the persistence of a mind or soul after death must be regarded as a logical possibility. Most religions, both in the East and the West, seek some type of immortality in their narrative, perhaps to soften the stark and inescapable reality of death. In Buddhism (the teachings of the Buddha), a new human life at the moment of conception (an embryo) is the union of three components: the sperm from the father, the ovum or egg from the mother, and a packet of consciousness derived from the universe. It is this packet of consciousness that we embellish, augment, or sometimes tarnish during our mortal existence and that we eventually return to an unknown dimension in the world. The mysterious emergence of genius from seemingly nowhere—Wolfgang Amadeus Mozart composing at the age of five; Srinivasa Ramanujan, who discovered the most profound theorems about numbers with no prior education—remains a mystery without some explanation of this general kind.

We shall discuss the role of Buddhism in the development of science in chapter 8. Suffice it to note here that through the enlightenment of the Buddha we have a description of human psychology that is distinctly post-Jungian. Buddhist psychology posits the existence of nine levels of consciousness—the five senses and four others. At the highest level of consciousness it is supposed that we actually connect with a universal consciousness, which can be viewed as the repository of all information in the cosmos, perhaps even predating the cosmos itself. Buddhist meditation—the practice of deep but detached introspection—endeavors to connect the individual with a consciousness of the universe. Ascetics, including the Buddha, apparently tapped into this reservoir of cosmic consciousness to achieve their enlightenment. When a scientist says that he had a sudden flash of insight in which he perceived a new way of understanding how the universe might fit together, this "inspiration" could be interpreted in the same manner as a transference of information already resident in some higher dimension of the universe—knowledge acquired by a process akin to meditation, the practice of mindfulness.

Recently researchers have found that Buddhist meditation can have a beneficial effect on patients who are recovering from cancer (Barash 2014). Remarkably, changes in DNA of a protective nature were found in these patients after several months of meditation but were absent in the control group. The mechanism by which meditation, consciousness, and the DNA of cells comes to be connected is as yet unknown.

Telepathy, the power to communicate by "transmission" of thought, has been written about for over half a century. Many allegedly controlled experiments are supposed to have demonstrated its feasibility. One story in circulation today involves astronaut Edgar Mitchell, who walked on the moon in 1971. He reports that he used telepathy successfully to communicate with friends while he was on Apollo 14 and they were on Earth. Their replies, also via telepathy, were received instantaneously, even defying the limitation imposed by the speed of light!

We conclude this chapter with the remark that the precise relationship between a presumed cosmic consciousness and individual living entities still remains enigmatic. If the living entities have all their genes derived from viruses in the cosmos at large, one might speculate that consciousness also has a cosmic provenance.

CHAPTER 5

VIRAL FOOTPRINTS IN THE EVOLUTION TO *HOMO SAPIENS SAPIENS*

Somewhere in the steaming jungles of the Carboniferous Period there emerged an organism that for the first time in the history of the world had more information in its brains than in its genes. It was an early reptile, which, were we to come upon it in these sophisticated times, we would probably not describe as exceptionally intelligent. . . . Much of the history of life since the Carboniferous Period can be described as the gradual (and certainly incomplete) dominance of brains over genes.

CARL SAGAN, *THE DRAGONS OF EDEN: SPECULATIONS ON THE EVOLUTION OF HUMAN INTELLIGENCE*

Bacterial cells, known by the term *prokaryotes* (or *prokaryotic cells*), have no nuclei or internal structures within them. The cells of all higher life-forms (eukaryotic cells) contain nuclei as well as internal structures known as mitochondria (in animal cells) and chloroplasts (in plant cells). These structures are vital for performing the more varied and complex functions of higher life-forms. Mitochondria produce the energy currency of the cell, the molecule called ATP, by capturing energy through respiration. Chloroplasts are similarly responsible for harnessing light energy from sunlight to make sugars through the process of photosynthesis. There has been much speculation as to when, how, and why these apparently hybrid cells arose.

There is now scarcely any doubt that the large-scale shift from predominantly prokaryotic cells on Earth (directly supplied from space, in our view) to eukaryotic cells arose sometime around 1.7 to 2 billion years ago. The big question then relates to the extraordinarily long time lapse between the first emergence of bacterial life on Earth (4.3 billion years ago) and the emergence of eukaryotes. For an Earth-bound theory of evolution, this constitutes a major difficulty. For neo-Darwinian evolution involving the accumulation of random copying errors in DNA followed by natural selection, the 2 billion year time lapse is implausibly long.

How this happened is still in the realm of guess work, but the most popular view is that prokaryotes gave rise to the first eukaryotic cells by a process known as endosymbiosis. Mitochondria and chloroplasts began as bacteria that became engulfed within the larger cells to function as single combined entities. This step opens the way to the evolution of all plants and animals.

Chloroplasts and mitochondria are just two of the many different types of organelles in eukaryotic cells, and all these entities are most likely to have originated as bacteria that initially served a cooperative role in cell function as symbionts while still existing as independent entities.

The present-day role of symbiotic microorganisms, particularly in the human gut, has been recognized for many years (Wickramasinghe et al. 2015). The understanding of the overwhelming importance of the human microbiome, with an estimated total bacterial count of ~10^{14} (one hundred trillion) individual cells, has been relatively recent

(Turnbaugh et al. 2007). Advances in gene sequencing techniques have made it possible to obtain a better understanding of this somewhat enigmatic entity, although its origin, maintenance, and long-term evolutionary impact remains unclear (NIH HMP Working Group et al. 2009; Qin et al. 2010).

Automated gene sequencing techniques have yielded a total number of genes associated with our human microbiome that grossly exceeds the twenty-two thousand or so protein-coding genes in the entire human genome. A large fraction of these genes may be of viral rather than bacterial origin. A consortium of researchers has recently published a gene catalogue of 3.3×10^6 nonredundant genes in the microbiome of the human gut. Because gene sequence mapping does not distinguish between viruses, plasmids, and transposable genes, the viral component in the microbiome may perhaps be the most significant.

The human gut microbiome has often been described as the most densely populated ecosystem on Earth. Included are many groups of extremophiles, including acidophiles, both symbiotic and pathogenic, that are significantly different from free-living microbial populations. Most importantly, they have the ability to transfer viral particles (virions) to invading bacteria and thereby offer a system of defense. The remarkable individuality and time variability of the human microbiome, particularly in the gut (Turnbaugh et al. 2007), has come as a surprise to investigators in recent years. Its possible role in health, immunity, and disease is only just coming to be recognized by physicians.

How did the human (and other) microbiomes arise in the first place? Are they the outcome of millions of years of coevolution between evolved organisms (mammals, humans) and an ever-changing population of environmental bacteria and viruses? In our view the population of microbial and viral entities identifiable with microbiomes is being continuously replenished and augmented from space.

It is known that a single drop of ocean water contains more than ten million individual virus particles. On this basis we can arrive at a total count of 0.5–1×10^{10} virions per liter or $\sim 10^{31}$ virions throughout all the oceans of Earth. The possibility that microbiomes associated with animals are acquired, at least in part, from this pool of viruses—cosmic viruses in our view—cannot be ignored.

It is a sobering thought that if not for these humble cosmic viruses none of us would ever have been born. In 2000 a team of scientists discovered an unfamiliar gene in the human genome (Mi et al. 2000). The gene coded for a protein called syncytin, which is made only by cells in the placentas of mammals. What is more, such cells were found only where the placenta made contact with the uterus. They fused together to form a single membrane called the syncytiotrophoblast. The syncytiotrophoblast is vital for the survival of the unborn fetus and is involved in extracting nutrients from its mother. What is remarkable about syncytin is that it is not a typical human gene but carries all the hallmarks of a viral gene. More recent studies have shown that this gene is present not only in humans but also occurs in all primates. We could thus surmise that viral ingress transporting the syncytin gene from space gave rise to the emergence of placental mammals on our planet.

When the entire human genome was first sequenced in 2001, it was discovered that of the three billion or so base pairs in the human genome, less than a percent code for protein, leading to a total of some twenty-five thousand protein-coding genes. The discovery came as a surprise. Lurking within our protein-coding DNA are vast arrays of noncoding DNA derived from so-called retroviruses, presumably relics of cosmic RNA viruses that had invaded our planet millions of years ago.

Retroviruses (which include HIV) have an enzyme called reverse transcriptase that has the property to transcribe their RNA into DNA after entering a cell. These vast sequences of retroviral DNA spliced into our ancestral genomes are by no means inert and mere junk DNA, as they were once thought to be. They serve as a store of long-term evolutionary potential, exactly as proposed many years ago by Hoyle and Wickramasinghe (1982) (see also Steele, E. J. et al. 2018, 2019).

On a much shorter timescale, retroviruses are responsible for ongoing gene regulation—the switching on and off of genes. Very recently it has been discovered that some retroviral DNA (in endogenous retroviruses, or ERVs) came to be integrated in regions of the human genome that regulate genes in the brain and may even have a role to play in intelligence and the emergence of *Homo sapiens sapiens.* Perhaps the greatest insight into the evolution of language has come from work on the FOXP2 gene based on studies of a London-based family by Simon Fisher and his colleagues at the University of Oxford in 2001.

Fisher began to look at the genomes of members of a single family straddling several generations—each one exhibiting serious speech impairment as well as difficulties with sentence construction and grammar. Fisher discovered that in all these cases a single mutation of a particular gene—the FOXP2 gene—was involved. This gene is now known to play a key role in language and vocalization, and tracking it through the development of the primate lineage allows us to explore the changes involved in the evolution of complex language.

While the role of the FOXP2 gene in brain development and function is now clear, other retroviruses—even some still undiscovered retroviruses—can be involved in tweaking our behavior in subtle ways. Another retrovirus that affects brain function and neurological disease is the borna virus, belonging to the Bornaviridae family of viruses. This virus is known to infect both mammals and birds, affecting them in different ways. However, very little is known of the mechanism by which the virus acts. In some species the virus appears to be harmless but in others not. Borna disease, which was first described more than two hundred years ago in Germany as a fatal neurologic disease of horses and sheep, derives its name from the town of Borna in Saxony, where a large number of horses died during an epidemic in 1885. The virus clearly affects the functioning of the brain. The horses go into wild fits and often kill themselves by smashing their skulls; in other instances they starve to death. There have been claims, not universally accepted, that borna viruses can silently alter human behavior, being implicated in conditions such as schizophrenia.

The borna virus has now been found to be present in every human on Earth. In the January 7, 2010, issue of *Nature,* a team of Japanese and American scientists have shown that the human genome does, indeed, carry borna virus genes (Horie et al. 2010). This retrovirus gained ingress into the genome of our ancestors some forty million years ago, and its genes have been transmitted to us in the present day.

It is generally agreed that a virus or bacterium could acquire new characteristics, not only from random mutations but also by incorporating new genetic sequences from ambient virions—viruses from space. The Zika virus appears to have undergone precisely such a change in recent years. Before 2000, the Zika virus was in circulation but did not cause microencephalitis in newborn babies; this suggests a major change in the virus. The altered Zika virus, which is now spreading in many countries via a mosquito vector, has been found to affect fetuses in pregnant women, causing babies to be born with reduced brain and skull size. It is also of interest to note that at least one case of transfer of the virus to gametes has been noted in an infected male. The isolation of the virus in semen may be an indication of the soma-to-germline feedback process already occurring in this instance (Steele 2016). More cases of a similar kind are to be expected, and the situation is similar to the seminal transmission mode of HIV when it exploded on the scene unexpectedly in 1981. The Zika epidemic, if it proceeds unchecked, could eventually lead to the emergence of a new human phenotype with reduced brain size and greatly diminished cognitive capacity. It is to be hoped, however, that modern medical science will intervene in time to prevent such a tragic outcome.

Luis Villarreal has argued that viral footprints can be identified in human brain tissue and that these mark important steps that led up to its present condition. The possibility that Zika-virus-induced microcephaly might represent a retrogression of this trend is an alarming prospect that medical science would have to avert before it is too late (Villarreal 2004). On a more positive note, many similar viruses with unknown disease potential or evolutionary opportunities—perhaps to higher levels of cognition and intelligence—may well be lurking within our genomes at the present time. One such virus may perhaps be involved in the recognition of our cosmic origin—our reawakening in the fullness of time.

CHAPTER 6

UNBRIDLED GREED— A COSMIC IMPERATIVE?

Primitive men, and to a large extent also men of the early civilizations, imagined themselves to be living on a virtually illimitable plane. . . . The image of the frontier is probably one of the oldest images of mankind, and it is not surprising that we find it hard to get rid of.

KENNETH E. BOULDING,
BEYOND ECONOMICS

This statement above by Kenneth E. Boulding was published in his book *Beyond Economics* in 1968. In 1972 the Club of Rome published his book titled *The Limits to Growth,* in which he raised an alarm relating to the consequences of the exponential growth of population and consumption, concluding that the limits to growth on this planet will be reached within the next hundred years.

In this chapter, which the reader might think is a diversion from our main narrative, we speculate on the existence of a virus-driven gene imperative that might explain some seemingly illogical and enigmatic aspects of human behavior. Why did the evolution of *Homo sapiens* not come with an innate wisdom to preserve our planet and the future well-being of our own species? Why do we so callously engage in conduct that is manifestly unwise and damaging? It seems that we are trapped in some bizarre genetic program to self-destruct. And if so, is this not inconsistent with the tenets of purely Earth-bound neo-Darwinism?

In 1798 Thomas Malthus (1766–1834) set the cat among the pigeons in the world of politics with his book *An Essay on the Principle of Population.* Here he proposed that whenever there was a rise in the level of prosperity, food production also increased and so did people's fertility. Unbridled consumption then leads inevitably to a rise of population with a consequent decline of living standards that in turn leads to social unrest, revolution, and war.

All the alarms that have been raised from the time of ancient civilizations to the late eighteenth-century Malthusian arguments on the impossibility of unlimited growth have gone unheeded. We seem to possess a naive expectation that some kind of supertechnological miracle will appear and solve the issue of limitation of human progress. This hope will remain as an illusory irrational hope—not so much due to the limits of nonrenewable natural resources but because of irreversible pollution caused by their use.

Undoubtedly the most dangerous and serious sources of pollution, which pose a grave threat with negative impact on Earth to most plants and animals, including humans, are the spent nuclear fuels already piled up in countries that have operated nuclear plants to generate electric energy. As of 2007, the spent nuclear fuels inventory of the top ten countries amounted to approximately 174,500 metric tons. This converts to about 5,235 metric tons of TRU (trans-uranic waste), which in turn translates to about 6×10^{23} becquerels of ionizing radiation, as each metric ton of TRU radioactivity is about 3 billion curies. This TRU needs to be kept safely isolated from all life on Earth for more than one hundred thousand to one million years until the ionizing radiation risk is reduced to 0.1 to 1 percent. There is no technology, chemical reaction, or physical interference available or even on the horizon today that can diminish the radioactivity of the spent nuclear fuels. We can only wait for more than a hundred thousand years and hope that some kind of natural calamity will not disturb its isolation.

The danger from the spent nuclear fuels is the internal radiation more than the external radiation. External radiation can be avoided and its effects reduced by staying as far away from the source of radiation as possible. Internal radiation, on the other hand, once taken into the body through food, water, and air, forces daily exposures until the time that radiation substances are excreted from the body. The effects of radiation in causing tissue damage and gene destruction mutations are significant (DNA binding is only a few eVs). The total mass of seawater is estimated at 1.37×10^{21} liters. A simple calculation implies that if all the accumulated spent nuclear fuels are someday dumped by force of nature or human will into the oceans, the average radiation level of the seawater will be about 438 becquerels per liter of water. This is about four thousand times higher than the maximum permissible level (0.11 becquerels per liter) of cesium 137 of the United States' drinking water. The radioactive substances in the ocean would be concentrated by plankton, sea plants, and sea animals by factors of one hundred to one million, so if the radioactive substance dumping becomes a reality we will have to abandon any contacts with the ocean. This, therefore, is the largest immediate threat to all biology on Earth.

The question then is why we cannot depart from our growth-oriented life and pursue a lifestyle more in harmony with nature. This remains a puzzle despite all the writing on the wall, which has been clearly visible for more than ten thousand years, and the prognostications of so many great individuals.

We humans have evolved, it seems, to crave the use of the non-renewable natural resources of Earth and to consume without replenishing them. This appears to be a "cosmic imperative" or a "cosmic will," an inescapable fact, which we subconsciously conceal.

In our view most of evolution and consequently all emergent

biological traits are due to the acquisition of cosmic viruses and are therefore predetermined. The tendency of most species on Earth to live at a subsistence level, while only a tiny minority (humankind) aspires to unbridled profligacy in expending nature's bounty must also be conditioned by externally driven viruses and virions. In this chapter we explore the bold speculation that there are two broad classes of species-generating viruses. The first class of viruses, which are in the vast majority, is directed to the generation of living species that are frugal in their use of planetary resources (life-economical, by Le); the second is a minority of viruses producing creatures like ourselves that can be described as profligate (life-uneconomical, or Lu). In what follows we use the descriptions Le, Lu to denote two categories of *presumed* virally acquired characteristics: the former that subsists in harmony with a planetary ecology, and the latter that does not.

From the entire spectrum of life-forms present on Earth, a clear division exists in regard to their use and expenditure of energy. The vast majority of species from the three domains of life—archaea, bacteria, eukaryotes—may be described as "energy economical," implying that only such energy is consumed as is needed to maintain life. The latecomers on the scene, the last mammals, which are ourselves, *Homo sapiens sapiens,* merit the description of being energy profligate, those who are obstinately determined to expend the nonrenewable natural resources of a planet, Earth, with little regard for conservation and pollution. This is easily seen in the fact that the average energy consumption by modern humans is 47,400 kilocalories per day, per person, which is some twenty-four times more than the bare survival energy consumption rate of ~2,000 kilocalories per day per person. Another way of interpreting the division between the two life-forms, Le and Lu, is that Le is dependent on reaping the direct energy of solar radiation, whereas Lu consumes the stored reservoirs of solar energy.

In order to understand the reason that we (Lu) refuse to live in harmony with other life-forms on Earth (Le), let us begin by surveying the development of our ancestral line as it has been revealed by modern gene sequencing. First of all, we should note that our phylogenetic links have now been traced back to fungi that emerged some 700 to 1,000 million years ago. At this early stage our distant ancestors, along with other life-forms, expended only the barest minimum of the energy and resources needed for maintenance and reproduction.

About seven million years ago our ancestral evolutionary line diverged from that of chimpanzees living in trees, and our ancestors started to walk upright on two legs (e.g., *Sahelanthropus, Ardipithecus, Australopithecus*) with the ability to use their hands to make tools. Not long afterward, 2.5 million years ago, *Homo habilis* emerged, and about 1 to 1.5 million years ago *Homo erectus* exploited the use of fire, and this led eventually to the exploitation of energy sources based on wood, coal, oil, gas, and ultimately uranium and plutonium in the present day. Until this time, we (Lu) had been content to survive on the minimum ration of 2,000 kilocalories of energy per day per person, or less, living along in perfect harmony with other life-forms (Le) and our planet Earth itself.

A crucial turning point in the fortunes of Earth as well as of humans may have occurred about fifty thousand years ago when *Homo sapiens sapiens* suddenly acquired a set of genes, including the FOXP2 gene, that enabled them to use words and develop language. This crucial development enabled us (Lu) to transmit ideas, engage in discourses, and ultimately discover and accumulate knowledge and experience, leading to science and modern technology. From this moment onward, *Homo sapiens sapiens* abandoned the energy-limited way of life of the Le and began to consume more and more energy—vastly more than was required for basic maintenance. The invention of language led to the invention of money, the most powerful tool of man, since it is directly tied to his greed. Money has evolved from a convenient medium of exchange to the highest status as the most suitable medium to reserve our greed. Thus *Homo sapiens sapiens* entered the path of the Lu, dictated, as we surmise, by the life-uneconomic suite of cosmic viruses.

In the millennia that followed, societies, kingdoms, and nation-states came into being along with economic systems that basically determined the distribution of wealth. All these developments apparently betrayed the natural order of the living world on the planet Earth. "Tradition" was the rule of survival in the most primitive hunter-gatherer societies, where the head of the family determined the distribution of wealth (the catch). The rule of survival then shifted to "command" in agriculture societies, where the head of the society, the king, decided on the distribution of the harvest. This order of things prevailed as long as the centralized control provided the cohesive force necessary to maintain a stable society. The fall of the Roman Empire in 476 CE may illustrate the result of decentralizing such a single hierarchical system into a multiplicity of hierarchical units on a global scale. Thereafter "command" was finally predominately replaced by "laissez-faire" (free for all), which still dominates most capitalist economies of the present day.

The misconception that a profit to an individual is ultimately good to society (the philosophy of materialism: enrich yourselves, the path to peace) under the laissez-faire system emancipated and approved greed as a virtue into the society. It harnessed the unlimited pursuit of profit and accumulation of wealth by the Lu-dominated lifeform. This society is referred to as a "cowboy economy" by Kenneth E. Boulding. It is an open economy with no limits. In his words, "I am tempted to call the open economy the 'cowboy economy,' the cowboy being symbolic of the illimitable plains and also associated with reckless, exploitative, romantic, and violent behavior, which is characteristic of open societies" (Boulding 1968).

In contrast, a closed society is referred to as "spaceship economy," where reservoirs of anything for extraction and pollution are limited and where a cyclical ecological system must be established. This concept is repeated by Ernst Friedrich Schumacher in his book titled *Small Is Beautiful*. He writes, "To illustrate a very simple thesis: that economic growth, which viewed from the point of economics, physics, chemistry and technology, has no discernible limit, must necessarily run into decisive bottlenecks when viewed from the point of view of environmental science. An attitude to life, which seeks fulfillment in the single-minded pursuit of wealth—in short, materialism—does not fit into this world, because it contains within itself no limiting principle, while the environment in which it is placed is strictly limited" (Schumacher 1973).

Gandhi made it elegant and clear: "Earth provides enough to satisfy every man's need, but not for every man's greed."

There is no place in the cosmos at large for the greed and envy of Lu-determined creatures in a closed economy.

Comets and asteroids have struck Earth sporadically, causing a succession of episodes of extinction of species. One such event that happened sixty-five million years ago led to the extinction of the dinosaurs and may well have shot Le DNA and RNA back into space. We cannot predict when the next comet or asteroid impact will take place, but when it does (perhaps ten thousand years hence!), our genes, enhanced with Lu DNA and RNA could find their way back into space.

From their manifest properties, it could be said that the primary objective of viruses is replication and only replication (the more progeny the better). This seems to be their ultimate cosmic will. Of course, we *Homo sapiens sapiens* do not want to admit that. Such an implied attribution of purpose or predestiny would diminish our own self-determination as well as the role of "cause" for every phenomenon in the natural world. From what we have discussed above, it would appear that the nature of living forms on Earth is, indeed, predetermined to a large extent by what appear to be the intrinsic properties of the universe—those of the Lu group viruses in particular—meaning that we humans are living under the basic influence of the Lu group viruses, whose main objective is to mass multiply through the speedy and maximum use of energy stored in planets. The Le group of viruses and the species they generate, on the other hand, multiply by using only the energy provided to planets by their parent stars.

It is a historical fact that every time we relied on human wisdom we have been disappointed. In short, throughout the history of civilization, human wisdom and intelligence have failed to produce the expected results of ecological harmony and peace on this planet Earth. We must find the fourth rule of survival other than tradition, command, and laissez-faire, as discussed earlier, based on new scientific discoveries—namely panspermia—in unraveling the mysteries of the human genome.

Finally, we may have turned to economists to guide us to the fourth rule of survival. But that seems improbable in view of the fact that modern economics is firmly anchored on the concept of materialism and consequently on capitalist philosophy. Economics based on capitalism leads us to follow its command in a laissez-faire environment. The main belief of the capitalistic economy is very simple. It is to be economical and make money (profit). Therefore, making lots of money (profit) is very good. Accumulation of money (profit) to build wealth and multiplication of wealth are virtues leading to satisfaction (of greed), which therefore engenders peace. Peace is pursued by wealth because it is believed that wealth needs peace to secure more wealth. Of course, this is an unproven proposition so far.

The core concepts of economics are goods and their production, distribution, and consumption. All goods have a monetary value that is determined by the market. Everything therefore has a price. It is often difficult to set a price for a service or for other human attributes like emotions, so in such cases a cost/benefit ratio is applied to indirectly determine a price. Therefore everything, even happiness, can be bought with money. This principle has brought money to become the highest of all values. If money can buy anything, at any time of need, and if everything is forever available in any quantity, money is the best partner of our greed. Our biggest problem is that some of the most crucial goods, the nonrenewable resources and our wastebasket, are limited. Thus we need to control our greed, as residents of Earth, but as we all know, throughout our entire history we have never been able to do so.

The sickness of our society is the fact that we live on a finite-sized planet with finite resources, but we (Lu-dictated creatures), the current drivers of the planet, have an insatiable greed to deplete its resources as fast as possible. There is no respite in sight: our collective greed continues to escalate with no signs of diminishing. It may be because the cosmic will of the Lu genes is effectively in the driver's seat and telling us that we need to move on to the next planet! We do not belong here except as temporary tenants. We have refused to see the truth that we are energy monsters with the Malthusian determination to multiply and then to return to space as soon as possible, if only because there are trillions of other planets on which to live and multiply. A purely

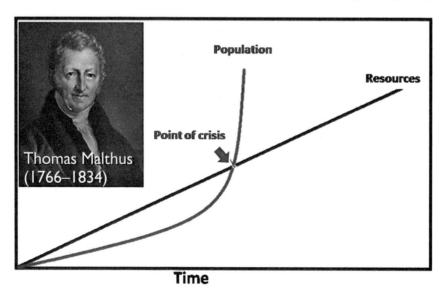

Fig. 6.1. Thomas Malthus—outstripping of resources with population growth

Earth-based solution may be extremely difficult and limited if such genetics are at work. If the genes, which determine us, put the Lu in action to consume Earth's limited nonrenewable resources, the workable terrestrial solutions will be crucially limited because we will need to act against our genetic will—our instinct. We can only hope, at least temporarily (as a holding operation), to admit our cosmic ancestry and cosmic will and impose on ourselves temporarily rules by which to live in harmony with other life-forms, the Le, on Earth.

CHAPTER 7

LESSONS FROM THE COPERNICAN REVOLUTION

The state of Ptolemaic (Earth-centered) astronomy was a scandal before Copernicus's announcement. Given a particular discrepancy, astronomers were invariably able to eliminate it by making some particular adjustment in Ptolemy's system of compounded circles. But as time went on, a man looking at the net result of the normal research effort of many astronomers could observe that astronomy's complexity was increasing far more rapidly than its accuracy and that a discrepancy corrected in one place was likely to show up in another.

THOMAS S. KUHN,
THE STRUCTURE OF SCIENTIFIC REVOLUTIONS

The most important intellectual revolution in the long history of civilization was perhaps the removal of Earth from its cherished place at the center of the universe. To our earliest ancestors living their lives on terra firma, an Earth-centered view of the world may have just seemed natural. As far as we can tell the first challenge of this position in Western philosophy came from the Greek philosopher Philolaus of Croton (470–385 BCE), who proposed that Earth and planets were not stationary and motionless but rotated around a central fire. The nature of the fire itself was left undefined. The ideas of Philolaus apparently remained ignored until nearly a century later, when Aristarchus of Samos (310–230 BCE) presented the first comprehensive heliocentric model of the universe, with the sun placed at the center and the planets, including Earth, revolving around it. Aristarchus was influenced by Philolaus but went further by identifying the central fire with the sun and also placing the other planets in their correct order of distance

Fig. 7.1. Aristarchus of Samos
(310–230 BCE)

around the sun. Aristarchus's ideas were ignored for over two thousand years, mainly on account of the powerful influence and authority of Aristotle and later of Ptolemy, who propagandized aggressively for a modified form of geocentric (Earth-centered) cosmology.

The revival of the correct heliocentric worldview after the Renaissance in Europe began with Nicolaus Copernicus (1473–1543). Copernicus was born to a wealthy merchant family in Torun, Poland. After his father died when he was just seven years old, he was taken under the wing of a maternal uncle who was the bishop of Varma. He arranged for the young Copernicus to receive the best possible education, which included mathematics, natural philosophy, Greek and Latin, and, of course, theology. His connection to the church almost certainly remained strong throughout his life. Apart from his uncle who was a bishop, his brother was an Augustine monk and his sister a Benedictine nun. Copernicus himself maintained a close relationship with the royal houses of both Prussia and Poland and thus indirectly maintained

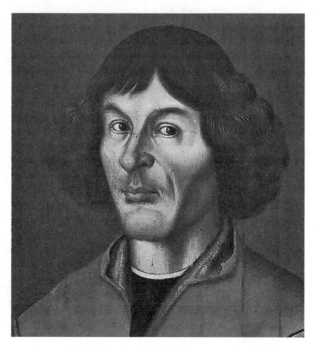

Fig. 7.2. Nicolaus Copernicus (1473–1543)

a connection with the church. It is against this strongly ecclesiastical backdrop that his amazing career has to be viewed.

There can be little doubt that Copernicus, with his background of a sound classical education, was well aware of earlier ideas that prevailed in Classical Greece. About two millennia earlier, a heliocentric model of the world was well documented through the published work of Philolaus and Aristarchus. It is therefore quite remarkable that Copernicus's publication *De revolutionibus orbium coelestium* of 1543 makes no reference whatsoever to either of these ancient writers. Owen Gingerich, a Harvard University historian of science, notes that an extant handwritten document of this book exists in which an extended paragraph referring to Aristarchus is crossed out (see fig. 7.3). In this case there is little doubt that Copernicus was well

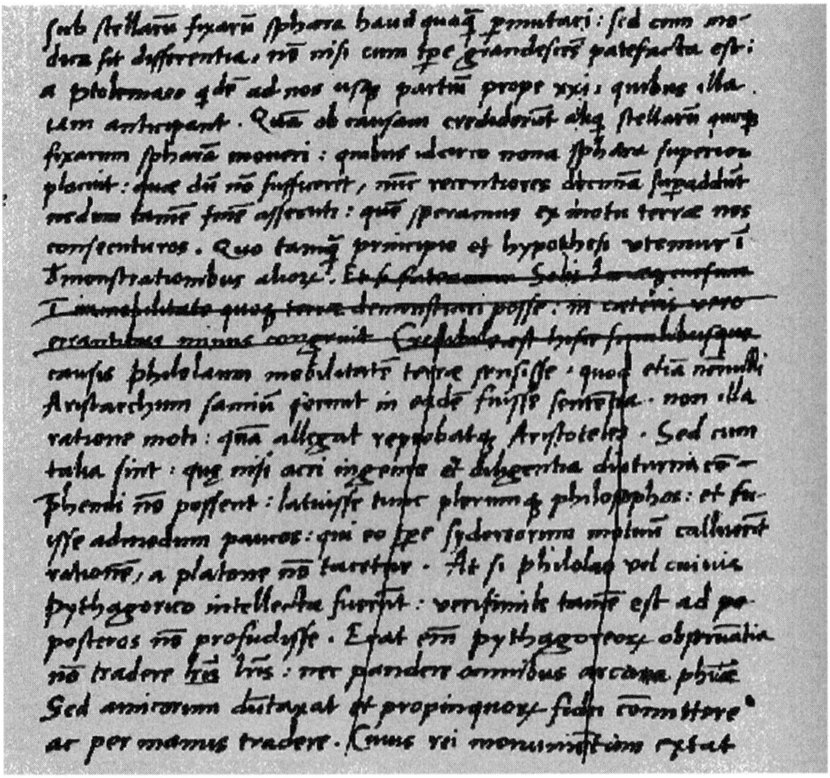

Fig. 7.3. Page from an original draft of De revolutionibus orbium coelestium

aware of this earlier work on a heliocentric universe but ignored it to strengthen the case for his own exclusive priority. There are also other indications to suggest that Copernicus was a somewhat intrepid yet reluctant revolutionary. He was well aware of the heresy associated with his idea and remained careful not to offend the church, to which he was closely connected. It is said that he did not proselytize for his heliocentric theory, not wishing to anger the church and perhaps to avoid ridicule and persecution. It is also significant that he put off the publication of his treatise until 1543, the year of his death. The reaction of the church when it was finally published was predictably muted. They expressed neither support nor hostility, but maintained that the heliocentric arguments were not convincing and moreover that they constituted heresy.

Throughout Copernicus's lifetime and for the next hundred years, heliocentric ideas failed to have any influence.

Some thirty years later, the German mathematician and astronomer Johannes Kepler (1571–1630) comes along. His father, who was a mercenary, left the family when Kepler was five years old and is thought to have died in battle. Kepler was brought up by his mother, who was evidently a healer and herbalist. She was later accused of witchcraft, and it is interesting to note that Kepler played a part in defending her in her trial and securing her freedom.

Kepler showed great gifts for mathematics and science from an early age and won a scholarship to the University of Tubingen, where he set out to study theology, aiming to become a Lutheran minister. It was during his time at the university that he came across the works of Copernicus. He reexamined the heliocentric theory in the light of new astronomical data and soon concluded that it must be substantively correct. The departure from the Copernican model, however, was that planets moved around the sun in ellipses, not circles—a seemingly minor departure but one that was to have an important bearing on our eventual understanding of the laws governing planetary

Fig. 7.4. Johannes Kepler (1571–1630)

motion. With his insight and genius, Kepler immediately brought the nascent heliocentric model of the universe to the fore. He influenced other contemporary astronomers, notably the Danish astronomer Tycho Brahe, to make better astronomical observations that firmly established the theory. Throughout his life Kepler remained a fervent Christian and believed that his studies could throw light on revealing God's purpose. In effect, he believed that he was a prophet of some kind whose destiny was to unravel God's building plans for the world.

Galileo Galilei (1564–1642) next enters the scene and, with his

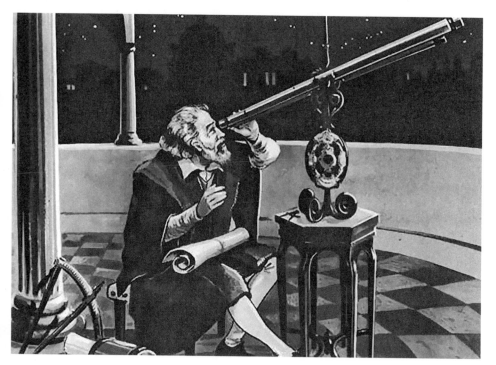

Fig. 7.5. Galileo Galilei
(1564–1642)

many scientific instruments and the use of a telescope, for the first time defends the heliocentric worldview. His observations and publications provoked the 1633 Inquisition that led to his being convicted of heresy. The statutory punishment for heresy was commuted to one of house arrest for the rest of his life upon his retraction of heliocentric theory. The interesting legend (which may be apocryphal) is that after affirming that he was wrong about a heliocentric world he is said to have looked down at his feet and muttered the words, "E pur si muove" (Albeit, it does move).

Perhaps the most famous martyr of the Copernican revolution is the Italian astronomer Giordano Bruno (1548–1600). Bruno, who supported the newly emerging heliocentric model of the solar system, proposed the existence of Earth-like planets around other stars—

exoplanets, as we now call them. For this heresy he was burned at the stake by a papal decree.

Isaac Newton (1642–1727) is the next player to enter the stage. Starting from Kepler's laws of planetary motion, he derived the law of universal gravity. Newton effectively showed how the force of gravity holds all the planets in their elliptic orbits around the sun. This marked the end and final conclusion of the Copernican revolution.

We have already discussed that the modern extension of the Copernican revolution—the quest to remove Earth from the center of biology—began in the 1970s with the efforts of one of us (CW) and the late Sir Fred Hoyle. This modern second phase of the Copernican revolution turned out to be every bit as acrimonious as the first, although the rules of conduct and engagement had evolved over the centuries.

In the twenty-first century perpetrators of heresy are silenced not by brutal executions but by a more subtle combination of ostracism and censorship. Publication of ideas that are disapproved of is promptly blocked from journals by a process that has come to be called peer review. Peer review at best means checking for factual and demonstrable errors; at worst it means attempting to preserve an ailing paradigm through brute force and censorship. Ideas unpalatable to an influential orthodoxy are thus banned from publication in prominent journals. Unorthodox lines of research are also starved of public funds and their practitioners ostracized in a multitude of ways.

The theory of cosmic life was not successfully stifled by any of these devices, however. Many of our earliest discoveries and arguments supporting panspermia were published in standard peer-reviewed journals, many in the journal *Nature*. The first outlet for our more radical ideas in the 1970s and 1980s took the form of commercial books. It is in this way that Hoyle and one of us (CW) arranged the publication of the classic trilogy—*Lifecloud, Diseases from Space,* and *Evolution from Space.* At a somewhat later date the internet and a range of open access journals offered scope for dissident scientists like ourselves to air our views. One way or another, the ideas we have discussed in this book could not be silenced, and the second phase of the Copernican revolution has come now to the verge of being accepted as part of mainstream science.

The complete and unconditional admission that the scientific facts across many fields demand a radical change in our thinking will, however, be resisted for a while. The methods used for this will range from point-blank denial of crucial facts to the propagation of false information designed to mislead. The motivation for such societal deception appears to be powerful. Possibly, it is a part of the cosmic condition that we have inherited from space but don't wish to admit. We shall discuss this in connection with the religious preconditioning of different cultures in the next chapter. Our cosmic connection, which we discussed in earlier chapters, implies that to a large extent we have no control of our own destiny. We are at the mercy of cosmic forces and cosmic imperatives, like a ship at sea blown hither and thither by the winds. A cosmic will always dominates.

Ever since the Industrial Revolution in the eighteenth century, we humans have become convinced that we are in absolute control of our destiny. We have come to believe, wrongly, of course, that our collective and largely benevolent will must always prevail. This is a proposition that has been falsified on many occasions: two devastating world wars, the horrors of fascism, Nazism, genocide in many parts of the world, and the decline of once-powerful empires. A succession of worldwide economic crises and our failure to alleviate world poverty make a mockery of what our twenty-first-century civilization should be.

Our present situation of arrogance and complacency is only going to get worse. Technological and economic progress is certain to continue more or less unabated, but sustainable development, which is still an empty catchphrase, will remain a distant goal. Maintaining a clean environment for future generations, compassion for the poor and needy do not seem to rank high on the list of priorities for the more powerful nations of the world. According to the United Nations, the world population today (2017) stands at 7.2 billion and is projected to increase by 1 billion over the next twelve years and reach 9.6 billion by 2050. Most experts agree that such a population rise is unsustainable, but they choose to do little or nothing about it. Will we have Malthusian interventions to check growth through a series of terrible catastrophes or devastating wars? This will be the inevitable future of our planet unless a radically new attitude prevails.

In any case, our cosmic connection is beyond refutation according to the new paradigm that is unfolding. Every evolutionary development of life, from the first emergence of multicellular life, the emergence of placental mammals, and finally the emergence of hominids and *Homo sapiens,* was predicated by a cosmic will delivered by viruses. All the pivotal steps in the progression leading from anthropoids to humans have unmistakable viral footprints that are only recently being discovered through modern gene sequencing. There is also tantalizing evidence that all lines of multicelled life came from comet-borne viruses that were brought to Earth 540 million years ago by an impacting cometary bolide.

Over the past decade there has been a gradual realization that life must be a truly cosmic phenomenon, and many people who were antagonistic to this idea in the past are beginning to voice contrary opinions about what should be done to cope with the realization that life exists outside Earth. In Davos, Switzerland, in 2014, the world's business leaders and politicians met to discuss global risks and challenges that would confront humanity in the next ten years. One of the top five global "risks" to be identified was the discovery of extraterrestrial life. This discovery, it is reckoned, would profoundly influence the entire future of humankind.

The prevalence of life of any kind outside our cozy Earth raises issues connected not only with science but also with security, psychology, sociology, and religion. To some religious groups the realization that the site of our "creation" was located outside Earth may cause conflicts with theology. Earth-centered theologies and philosophies may need to be revised.

The discovery of intelligent life outside Earth, if that happens, poses the most serious problems of all, calling for fundamental revisions and readjustments of our perceptions about ourselves. Even the mere proof that such extraterrestrial intelligence exists will seriously erode our perceived position of unrivaled supremacy in the world. And if an extraterrestrial intelligence is, indeed, found to be resident nearby, and contact thought imminent, the situation might become analogous to the fear that primitive tribes may have had regarding the prospect of encounters with more civilized conquerors.

CHAPTER 8

EAST IS EAST AND WEST IS WEST

*Oh, East is East and West is West, and never the twain
    shall meet
Till Earth and Sky stand presently at God's great
    Judgement seat.*

RUDYARD KIPLING,
THE BALLAD OF EAST AND WEST (STANZA 1)

Rudyard Kipling (1865–1936), who wrote these words, was an example of an unlikely union of cultures. Kipling was born in India (British India, as it then was), and his writings—the most famous being *Kim*—drew extensively from his experiences there. He was acclaimed as one of the finest prose writers of the day and was awarded the Nobel Prize for literature in 1907.

The British Empire, when Kipling was born, was the largest empire the world had seen. It followed a long succession of empires starting in the sixth century BCE with the Persians, Greeks, and Romans. While all these Western empires shared and spread a common cultural heritage, earlier empires had certainly existed elsewhere in Egypt, China, and India, but they remained to a large extent culturally separate. This is not to say that they existed in complete isolation, however. Trade routes and cultural connections did exist, but they remained vague and indistinct. We know, for instance, of the great Silk Route from China to the West, and it is clear that not only silk but also paper and printing, as well as gunpowder, came from China. It is also likely that many philosophical ideas, including concepts relating to mathematics, filtered into the West from India. The acknowledgment of these connections tends to be omitted, however, in most Western historical narratives, which tend to be fiercely Eurocentric and attempt to maintain an artificially imposed separation between East and West.

It is a remarkable fact that the emerging case for our cosmic connection and cosmic origin of life, which we have discussed in earlier chapters, had markedly different receptions in the East and West. When Fred Hoyle and one of us (CW) became sufficiently convinced that we were on the right track, it was decided that a crucial prediction of the theory was close at hand and had to be verified. If life came from comets four billion years ago, that process could not have stopped in the distant geological past because comets are, of course, still with us and continue to arrive here and interact with our planet. Microorganisms—bacteria and viruses—must therefore still be arriving from comets, and their continuing presence in the stratosphere is a definite prediction that urgently needed to be tested. Approaches were made to several space agencies and aerospace organizations in the West, but they met with no success.

Finally, it was the Indian Space Research Organization (ISRO) that came to the rescue in 2001. A collaboration between one of us (CW) and the ISRO was forged, and in 2001 material collected from the stratosphere at a height of 41 kilometers was recovered and examined in both the United Kingdom and India. Although a startling positive result was obtained—an estimated 0.1 tons of microbes arriving daily across the planet—the prompt refrain in the West was that our result *had to be dismissed* as likely contaminants. Or against incredible odds, the microbes we discovered in the high stratosphere were lofted from the ground. This is the response that was used to dismiss all later positive evidence for the theory of cosmic life, including a recent report by Russian cosmonauts of marine-type algae being discovered at a height of four hundred kilometers on the windows of the International Space Station.

That people believe what they want to believe is a truth more profound than it appears at first sight. Psychologists have recognized for a while the reality of a phenomenon that they call confirmation bias. We are constantly trying to reconfirm a prior notion we have in our brains about the world around us. This trait in humans gives us the comfort of security and may well be an inherited survival asset left over from our distant tribal ancestry.

If we have nothing personally at stake in evaluating two competing points of view—spontaneous generation and panspermia as just one example—we tend on the whole to be intelligent about assessing the validity of evidence objectively and reaching a rational conclusion. But if we, our friends, our kinsmen, or the science community at large have a stake in a particular outcome, impartiality becomes impossible, and we lose our ability to see any other side of an issue than our own. The more urgent the impulse, as in the defense of a cherished worldview, or the closer it comes to the maintenance of our own security, the more difficult it becomes to be rational.

Francis Bacon in 1620 wrote thus:

The human understanding when it has once adopted an opinion (either as being the received opinion or as being agreeable to itself) draws all things else to support and agree with it. And though there be a greater number and weight of instances to be found on the other side, yet these it either neglects and despises, or else by some distinction sets aside and rejects; in order that by this great and pernicious predetermination the authority of its former conclusions may remain inviolate. . . . And such is the way of all superstitions, whether in astrology, dreams, omens, divine judgements, or the like; wherein men, having a delight in such vanities, mark the events where they are fulfilled, but where they fail, although this happened much oftener, neglect and pass them by. (Bacon 1939)

Most new theories start life as guesses or speculations. Most do not survive rational analysis for long; experiments demonstrate that they are untenable.

According to Lakatos (1976), Newton's theory of gravitation was put forward as a bold guess that was ridiculed and even called "occult" by German philosopher Gottfried von Leibniz. But a few decades later—in absence of contrary evidence and with the fulfillment of predictions such as the return of Halley's comet—Newton's bold guess became an irrefutable law of nature. The earlier ridicule and suspicions were forgotten. Such is the nature of discovery when no insuperable ideological difficulties are faced.

In both the West and the East the history of ideas that relate to our place in the universe appears to have a direct or indirect connection with religion. Religion for the most part defines a worldview into which we attempt to fit all our experiences and our individual existence. So attempts to switch to an alternative or better worldview often come to be thwarted, falling into the category of confirmation bias that we have already discussed.

Early humans, *Homo sapiens*, struggled against a wide range of natural hazards in which survival was often perched on a razor's edge. The most primitive religious ideas were almost certainly linked to this struggle to cope with the most powerful forces of nature—droughts, floods, failure of crops. They provided the rationale for inventing gods of the wind, sea, and sky to whom supplication and loyalty was owed. A connection between human activities and the external cosmos must have been conceived in this way at a very early stage of our intellectual development.

The nearest approach to a rational or "correct" cosmic worldview must have been reached when humans invented the sun god. We know, of course, that the sun is, indeed, the source of all the heat, light, and energy that makes Earth a congenial planet on which to live. A solar deity correctly symbolizing power straddles the belief systems of many ancient cultures. Sun worship in ancient cultures can thus be seen as a pragmatic acknowledgment of our connection with our parent star.

The sun god acquired a multitude of different variants across the ancient world: Sol in German mythology, Helios to the Greeks, and the older Surya in Vedic traditions of India. Eventually, the adoption of distinct religious beliefs became a powerful source of group identity—hallmarks by which communities can be distinguished. With the passage of time, the simple fact of our allegiance to the sun and the wider cosmos became blurred in a superstructure of unprovable beliefs that essentially generated a great diversity of different religions. Heaven (the skies) becomes the abode of angels and deities in theistic religions—Judaism and Christianity, for instance. However, major differences emerged between Western and Eastern religions.

Hinduism, the indigenous religion of India, has roots (including Vedic traditions) that go back well before 2000 BCE. The beginnings of Judaism, on the other hand, can be fixed at around 1300 BCE. Judaism, and later Christianity and Islam, is a monotheistic religion—positing the existence of a single god. Hinduism, on the other hand, has a pantheon of gods and goddesses, each carrying out different functions or representing different aspects of our existence: Brahma, the Creator; Vishnu, the Preserver; Shiva, the Destroyer; Ganapati, the Remover of Obstacles; Saraswati, the Goddess of Learning; Lakshmi, the Goddess of Wealth. It is difficult to resist the speculation that these many gods of Hinduism are, in fact, different aspects of a single god, or even, perhaps, they can be seen simply as metaphors for the many different aspects of human aspirations.

In stark contrast to these theistic religions, we find Jainism and

Buddhism appearing in India in the fifth century BCE, both of which deny the existence of a deity. It is remarkable that these developments in India coincide in timing with similar developments in the Mediterranean world. The fifth century BCE appears to have been a period of worldwide ferment and cultural reawakening. Earlier religious beliefs came under rigorous scrutiny. In Athens we have Anaxoragas (510–428 BCE) pronouncing that the sun and moon are not gods but mere natural bodies. And then we have Democritus (460–370 BCE) with his theory of atomism, as well as Socrates (470–399 BCE) and Plato (428–348 BCE), whose ideas we have already discussed. At the same time in India, we have the Buddha (Gautama Siddharth) (563–485 BCE), and in China we have Confucius (551–479 BCE). The common feature of all these thinkers is that they questioned a traditional belief in a god or gods, transferring focus from an external agency to the inner self and thus to self-reliance.

Judaism, Christianity, and later Islam all shared a central belief in a single omnipotent god, with the implied assertion that the human (*Homo sapiens sapiens*) was the purpose of creation. As we discussed in the last chapter, until the middle of the seventeenth century, practitioners of these theistic religions believed that Earth was the center of the universe. The idea was of a geocentric cosmos, the stars and planets with their complex motions being mere ornaments in the heavens. The history of science in Europe appears to have been a continual challenge of religious views. One could, perhaps, argue that Western science flourished precisely because it had to confront authoritative assertions that were manifestly wrong.

When decisive evidence eventually came to be presented, the geocentric ideas were abandoned, although not without struggle and, indeed, bloodshed. We saw that Galileo Galilei was condemned by the Inquisition of Rome and placed under house arrest; Giordano Bruno was burned to death. Galileo's crime was that he said Earth moves around the sun; Bruno's crime was that he went against the church to proclaim that there may be inhabited planets orbiting other stars. Now we know that such habitable planets exist in their billions or trillions in the universe. But in 1600 Bruno's assertion was based on his intuition and his belief in the Copernican worldview.

We have already noted that philosophical and religious concepts that should long ago have been abandoned still persist, continuing to hinder the progress of science. We referred in particular to the Aristotelean idea of spontaneous generation, which is still very difficult to shake off because of its deep-rooted religious connection.

When an omnipotent creator-god is excluded, the resulting worldview, which is atheistic, becomes remarkably close to that offered by Buddhism, the fourth major religion in the modern world (along with Islam, Christianity, and Judaism). The architect of this religion was the Buddha. Buddha (as he is now referred to) was born as Gautama Siddharth (ca. 563–485 BCE) near Nepal in India. He relinquished the comforts of worldly life and sought answers to perennial questions relating to our existence and the nature of the human condition, and in particular he strove to understand the cause of suffering. He sought answers not by any religious practice or divine revelation but by meditation or deep introspection, a process in which his mind was transported through various levels of consciousness—eventually reaching the highest state of "enlightenment." What he discovered in this sublime state forms the basis of Buddhism. The Buddha's teachings—or dharma—expound the truth about the nature of the human condition and the universe, as well as the cause of suffering.

Buddhism offered a code of conduct to achieve liberation from human suffering. It recognized that most suffering is due to greed, envy, and the desire for attachment to worldly things. The code of conduct was encapsulated in the Eightfold Noble Path:

Right Understanding
Right Thought

Right Speech
Right Action
Right Livelihood
Right Effort
Right Mindfulness
Right Concentration

This code of conduct is not fundamentally different from the biblical Ten Commandments, but it exists without the context of belief in an almighty god. In its place, the belief in the law of karma gives an incentive to be kind and virtuous because all our actions have a bearing on our future destiny.

After Buddha's death, a monastic tradition developed that preserves and spreads his teachings. Buddhism as a social movement can be seen as a great equalizer and more specifically as a rebellion against the rigid Hindu caste system that had prevailed in India for thousands of years. Buddha's message of universal love and compassion for all life has resonated down the centuries and been a great civilizing force for humanity. In contrast to earlier religions that deferred ultimate judgment and all creative power to an all-powerful deity, Buddha's message was to take charge of your own lives and your destiny. In this sense Buddhism was a self-help religion. Through the process of mindfulness and meditation each of us could effectively interrogate the external universe and unravel its deepest secrets. Each of us is fully capable of reaching a mental state not far removed from Buddha's enlightenment or awakening.

Although the primary aim of Buddha's quest was to understand the cause of suffering, Buddhist scriptures are far more exhaustive in their scope. They include expositions of human psychology as well as of cosmology. Of particular relevance in the context of the present book is a passage in the Paranibbana Sutra, the Buddha's last words to his disciple Ananda:

Therefore, O Ananda,
Be ye lamps unto yourselves
Rely on yourselves alone, do not rely on others.
Hold fast to the Lamp of Truth.
Seek salvation only in the Truth.
Look not for help to anyone besides yourselves.

What a wonderful piece of advice! If this advice were heeded in the modern world (and alas, it is not), we would not be in the mess we are. The world would surely be a much better place. And as far as science is concerned, we would not have all the ego-related impediments for accepting the true nature of things, including, of course, our true cosmic origins.

On the specific matter of alien planets and alien life, the Buddha's insight seems to have led to a remarkable unraveling of a post-Copernican worldview a millennium before Copernicus. In a Buddhist text dated around the first century CE, the following statement is made: "As far as these suns and moons revolve shedding their light in space, so far extends the thousandfold universe. In it are thousands of suns, thousands of moons, and Earths and thousands of higher worlds that constitute the minor world system. . . . Hundred thousand such minor world systems constitute the intermediate world system. . . . Hundred thousand intermediate world systems constitute the major world system."

The latter references are to extraterrestrial abodes of life. The hierarchical structure of billions of stars and galaxies appears to agree neatly with modern astronomical knowledge.

To conclude this chapter we note that theistic religions, like powerful states, exert social control and, indeed, the control of ideas through fear of punishment. In Judaic traditions the fires of hell epitomized an ultimate punishment, while the wrath of the gods played an important role in maintaining discipline in pagan, Hellenistic, and early Roman cultures. In Hinduism, placating the gods also played an important role, and so also did the rigidly enforced caste system that preserved religious authority as well as law and order.

In a nontheistic religion such as Buddhism the rewards or consequences in a future birth (or incarnation) may be a substitute for divine reward, but it has never been a comparable force for maintaining social order and cohesion. In India Buddhism remained a minor religion from the time of the Buddha's death in circa 485 BCE to the third century BCE. In 268 BCE, after a bloodthirsty battle and victory at Kalinga, King Asoka converted to Buddhism and conquered the rest of his vast empire India, not through military power, but by the compelling force of Buddhist ideas. His benevolent reign for the next thirty-six years stands out in human history as a remarkable example of the power of ideas over military might. As could be imagined, however, an empire based on such idealistic principles and self-imposed discipline turned out to be fragile, and India reverted to Hinduism scarcely two generations after Asoka's death. The enduring legacy of Asoka, however, was his role in spreading Buddhism throughout Southeast Asia, making it the major world religion it has become today.

CHAPTER 9

THE THREAT OF COMETARY MISSILES

And bay trees in our country are all withered
And meteors fright the fixed stars of heaven
The pale-faced moon looks bloody on earth
And lean-looked prophets whisper fearful change.

WILLIAM SHAKESPEARE, *RICHARD II*

The first half billion years of Earth's history as a planet were riddled with frequent impacts by comets and asteroids. The collisions during this epoch essentially represented the final stages of the formation of Earth. Although this initial impact-dominated period, known as the Hadean epoch, came to an end about four billion years ago, collisions with comets and fragments of comets did not come to a complete halt. We have seen in earlier chapters that this continuing interaction with comets led to the delivery of life in the form of bacteria and viruses, and eventually to the evolution of all complex life on our planet.

There is now little doubt that the extinction of the dinosaurs and of over 75 percent of all genera of plant, animal, and microbial life occurred sixty-five million years ago as a result of a cometary impact. A process of this kind was first suggested by Hoyle and one of the present authors (CW) as early as 1978 (Hoyle and Wickramasinghe 1978a), and hard evidence for this was discovered a few years later by the father-and-son team of Luis and Walter Alvarez. The evidence came in the form of the discovery of high amounts of the metal iridium in rock deposits belonging to this period.

Other large-scale extinctions of species at earlier times have also been recorded and found to be associated with similar enhancements of iridium in geological sediments, signaling a cometary connection. Significant peaks in the extinctions of species have been discovered in the geological record at approximately 1.6, 11, 37, 66, 91, 113, 144, 176, 193, 216, 245, and 367 million years ago (fig. 9.1).

The entire pattern of mass extinctions of species over the past four hundred million years is strongly suggestive of recurrent catastrophic events of external origin occurring with a significant periodicity of about twenty-seven million years.

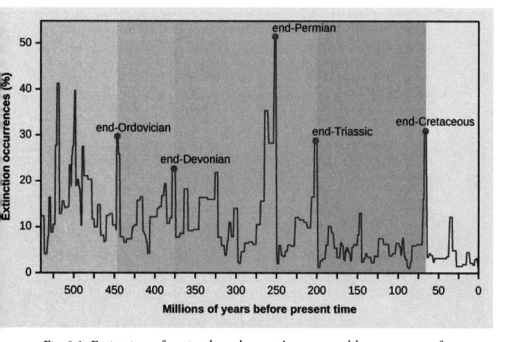

Fig. 9.1. Extinctions of species show sharp spikes separated by an average of twenty-seven million years.

We should not be content to think that dramatic effects of comet collisions are only confined to distant geological epochs. More recent episodes of comet and asteroid impacts have surely left their mark, not only as scars on the planet but on our history as well. To understand this process, it is important to recall what comets are made of. Recent studies have shown that comets possess relatively fragile internal structures that can be easily disrupted, leading to their sporadic breakup into a multitude of fragments.

Comets for the most part stay very far from the range of the inner planets, occupying orbits that envelop the planetary system at a distance of about a third of a light year from the sun. Occasionally, a comet swings past the giant planet Jupiter. When this happens, it is not only deflected in its orbit, so that it no longer returns to the most distant regions whence it came, it can also be shredded into pieces by the tidal forces exerted by Jupiter. This happened in the summer of 1992 for the now-famous Comet Shoemaker-Levy 9. The comet broke up into a string of some twenty-one pieces. In this case the pieces were all pulled in to become satellites of Jupiter, moving in orbits that slowly spiraled in toward the planet. Over the course of a single week in July 1994 all twenty-one pieces of Comet Shoemaker-Levy 9 crashed into Jupiter (fig. 9.2). This event provided a stark warning

Fig. 9.2. Comet Shoemaker-Levy 9 broke up into many fragments and collided with the planet Jupiter in 1994. (Image courtesy of NASA)

of the risks of collision that face all the planets of the solar system, including Earth.

The history of civilization, if it is correctly deciphered, in our view, bears witness to the most recent chapter of collisions with comets and fragments of comets, collisions that, in effect, controlled the fate of humankind, *Homo sapiens sapiens,* over the past tens of thousands of years. Our history is essentially punctuated by the effect of repeated episodes of Earth plowing through the debris of comets—and in particular plowing through swarms of fragments of one particular giant comet. We can provisionally identify this giant comet as a progenitor of Comet Encke, with its stream of debris connected with the Taurid meteor stream.

We estimate that the fragmenting giant comet (call it Comet X) may have weighed on the order of 10^{16} metric tons, one thousand to ten thousand times the mass of Halley's Comet, and measured about two hundred kilometers across. It would have become perturbed by Jupiter, say twenty thousand years ago, into a periodic orbit that crossed Earth's orbit. Within a few orbital revolutions around the sun fragmentation of the comet would have proceeded sequentially, giving rise to fragments of decreasing sizes, ranging from, say, ten kilometers to one hundred meters or less. On a ballpark estimate, the kilometer-sized pieces could number millions and the one-hundred-meter-sized pieces could number billions. All these pieces would remain bunched together within a single broad meteor stream that orbited around the sun, and Earth would go through this debris stream with some well-defined periodicity.

The average time interval between episodes of bunched collisions with debris is difficult to pin down to any degree of precision. Encounters could start with the initial orbital period of Comet X, but as the meteor stream disperses and evolves, the situation will become more chaotic. We shall now proceed to chart the progress of Comet X and its progeny (fragments) through time by attempting to identify crucial events in the history of our civilization that appear to be connected with possible cometary incursions. Fig. 9.3 gives a provisional timetable of historical events compared with the time interval of 1,500 years separating bunched collision events.

Each encounter will be characterized by a protracted episode of bunched collisions with cometary missiles—all of which are fragments of the original giant comet. During a bunched collision epoch, impacts of objects a few hundred meters across would pose a far greater threat than impacts of much larger pieces, which would occur far less frequently. Interactions with smaller fragments would have occurred with menacing frequency during the bunched collision epochs, each of which may have lasted several decades.

11,500 BCE	Earth engulfed in an ice age: Giant comet breaks up into fragments near Jupiter
10,000 BCE	First collision: Warm pulse
8,500 BCE	Second collision: Ice age ends
7,000 BCE	Bunched collisions
5,500 BCE	Bunched collisions: Agriculture begins
4,000 BCE	Bunched collisions: Discovery of copper smelting
2,500 BCE	Bunched collisions: End of Egyptian Old Kingdom; Pyramid building begins; Collapse of Mohenjodaro
1,000 BCE	Bunched collisions: Destruction of Jericho, Homeric Legends begin?
540 AD	Bunched collisions: Collapse of Roman Empire
2,040 AD	Bunched collisions again?

Fig. 9.3. Historical chart with a 1,500-year period superimposed

During the past twenty thousand years, the most important geological event was the emergence of Earth from the last ice age. This event may well have been triggered by impacts with cometary fragments. The process of unlocking the planet from its glacial state appears to have been accomplished in several stages.

The first stage of this process may have been caused by a collision with a large cometary fragment nearly 15,000 years ago. Earth suddenly warmed up but then cooled down again to remain intermittently glaciated for the next 3,000 years, during which minor temperature oscillations may have been caused by a succession of much smaller impacts that dispersed vast quantities of dust into the stratosphere that reflected sunlight and prevented a stable greenhouse from being established. It has recently been argued by some scientists that about 12,900 years ago Earth was, indeed, struck by thousands of one-hundred-meter size cometary fragments over a relatively short timescale, leading to a dramatic cooling of the planet. The cooling, by as much as 14°F (8°C), interrupted the warming that had begun and caused glaciers to readvance. It was exactly at this time, 12,900 years ago, that a prehistoric Paleo-Indian group known as the Clovis culture suddenly disappeared and ice-age animals such as ground sloths, camels, and mammoths also became extinct in North America. Recently, a team of researchers led by James Kennett has discovered melt-glass material in a thin layer of sedimentary rock in Pennsylvania, South Carolina, and Syria, pointing to the effect of cometary missiles striking Earth at this time.

A decisive emergence of Earth from the last ice age had to await a major collision event ten thousand years ago. Water that was released due to evaporation from the oceans by the heat of impact was sufficient to restore the greenhouse effect very quickly, thus causing Earth to pass into a stable warmer phase.

From this moment in time, at about 8000 BCE (ten thousand years ago), the history of human civilization might be said to have properly begun. At later times there is evidence of comparatively minor fluctuations in Earth's average surface temperature over timescales of centuries to millennia. Fluctuations above and below the present-day value occur in the general range of 3 to 6°F (~1.5–3°C). It is hard to find a purely Earth-based mechanism that could satisfactorily explain such a pattern. But again, impacts of cometary fragments provide a possible answer. Comets, frequently breaking up in the high atmosphere or in the near-Earth environment, would inevitably produce an increase in the dust loading of the stratosphere, thus enhancing the reflective power of the atmosphere to solar radiation. The result is that less sunlight gets through the atmosphere to heat the surface and more is reflected back into space, so cooling takes place.

For a typical cometary bolide with a diameter of about one hundred meters hitting Earth head-on at a speed of fourteen kilometers/second, the kinetic energy of impact is equivalent to about two metric megatons of the explosive TNT; that is, the equivalent of about a hundred bombs of the type that destroyed Hiroshima in 1945. Such an object, if made of ice, would explode at about thirty kilometers above the surface of Earth without any noticeable effect on human life. An object of only three times this size, a quarter of a kilometer in diameter, would strike much lower on Earth and cause localized destruction on a significant scale, perhaps on the order of a city. A larger cometary bolide with a diameter of a kilometer would have the energy of a hundred thousand Hiroshima bombs and would cause widespread damage, perhaps on the scale of an entire country. So the size of the incoming missile is the crucial factor that determines what the eventual outcome of a collision would be. The bigger the object, the greater the damage.

An object measuring about one hundred meters across entered the upper atmosphere of Earth over Tunguska in Siberia in the early hours of June 30, 1908. A great fireball was seen to pass low over the town of Kirensk and came down over a remote part of the Siberian taiga. The object did not reach the ground but exploded in the atmosphere at a height of about eight kilometers. The brilliant fireball, said to have outshone the sun, was seen as far as one thousand kilometers away from its point of descent, and the sound of the explosion was heard at even greater distances.

The immense blast wave that resulted from the explosion felled trees over a distance of some forty or fifty kilometers, and the heat from the fireball charred tree trunks for distances of up to fifteen kilometers from the center of impact. Estimates of the total energy of the impacting object range from thirteen to thirty metric megatons of TNT, which is equivalent to the explosive power of 650 to 1,500 Hiroshima bombs.

Collisions of the Tunguska type, and others on a much grander scale, must surely have occurred repeatedly throughout our history and prehistory for the past ten thousand years. If bunched collision episodes of our planet's encounters with the offending debris stream were separated by intervals of, say, 1,500 years, long periods of relative quiet may be seen to be interspersed by episodes of impacts lasting from ten to a hundred years.

The rise and fall of civilizations and the ascendancy and decline of empires that have punctuated human history over the last ten thousand years can be explained on the basis of these periodic assaults from the skies. The falls of civilizations would have occurred dramatically during short "bad periods" involving impacts, and the ascents to glory would have been maintained over longer periods of relative freedom from impacts.

Archaeological evidence shows that copper was being used for making tools and utensils at a date close to 4300 BCE. The first recorded use of pure copper is to be found in eastern Anatolia, but very quickly it spread across the world. The indication is that the relevant natural accident that produced copper smelting had to be repeated in several locations almost simultaneously. This was almost certainly multiple impacts of cometary bolides. Events of the Tunguska type during episodes of bunched collisions could have started forest fires on a huge scale. Beneath the intense heat of glowing charcoal, rocks containing appropriate metallic ores would have become naturally smelted. Our nomadic ancestors did not need any exceptional powers of observation to come across sites of smoldering forest fires similar to those that raged in Tunguska in 1908. They would only have had to pick up pieces of the smelted copper to discover that they could be beaten and flattened to yield artifacts that served their needs. This marked the beginning of the Copper Age, as it is sometimes called, which in turn led to the Bronze Age a thousand years later.

A well-documented episode or episodes of bunched collisions span the period from 2500 to 2300 BCE. Just before this time, several great civilizations and long-lived dynasties are known to have flourished, both in ancient Egypt and in the Indus River valley of northern India. The ruined city of Mohenjo-daro in northern Pakistan was the site of a pre-Aryan civilization that was perhaps more advanced than that of Egypt. It had flourished for over a millennium but suddenly and dramatically collapsed. Aryan invasions from the West could have produced a slow erosion of an already aging empire, but not a seemingly cataclysmic fall. Likewise, seasonal flooding of the Indus valley might have had a slow cumulative effect over many centuries but not a sudden one. A far more dramatic catastrophe could have arisen from tidal waves and tsunamis that follow quite naturally when cometary fragments crash into the sea. There has been recent evidence to suggest that a dust layer and a burned surface horizon, apparently caused by an air blast, exist in archaeological sites of northern Syria dated at about 2350 BCE.

Perhaps the strongest and most compelling evidence of an episode of cometary impacts is to be found in the deserts of Egypt. Following the unification of Upper and Lower Egypt by King Menes around 3100 BCE, a desert empire flourished, reaching heights of glory through a succession of dynasties of the so-called Old Kingdom of Egypt until its eventual collapse at about 2160 BCE. Pyramid texts describe a prolonged period of turmoil preceding the collapse. The construction of the three most famous Giza pyramids began with Snefru's son Khufu, who built the Great Pyramid around 2500 BCE. This stupendous structure has a base that covers some thirteen acres and a height of over 450 feet. The geometrical precision of the construction as well as the exact alignments of its faces to the cardinal points (north, south, east, and west) is remarkable to say the least. Two other major pyramids were built at Giza over the next two centuries by Khufu's son Khafre and his successor Menkaure.

Compelling evidence for a cosmic cataclysm that ended the Old Kingdom of Egypt comes from the work of scientists at Queen's University Belfast, led by Mike Baillie. They used the new science of dendrochronology, which involves the study of the thicknesses of annual tree rings at different times in the past. (Each year a new ring is formed in the trunks of trees, resulting from growth during the summer months.) A narrower tree ring corresponding to a particular year means that there was little or no tree growth during that year, which could only be explained as arising from greatly diminished levels of sunlight. Such a thinning of tree rings in Irish oaks has actually been discovered over the entire period from 2354 to 2345 BCE, which comes close to the final decades of the Old Kingdom. This is easily explained as being due to the arrival of Tunguska-type cometary missiles that dusted the atmosphere and dimmed the light from the sun.

The Epic of Gilgamesh is an epic poem from Mesopotamia dating back to before 2100 BCE (perhaps even earlier, to 2700 BCE) that was preserved on cuneiform tablets and is arguably based on real events. In the poem, Gilgamesh, king of Uruk, is depicted as the wisest of mortals with godlike attributes. He is reputed to have possessed great knowledge and wisdom, including information of "the days before the flood." The dating of the flood is open to question, but if he is identified as the historical king of Uruk, the date of the events described must come close to the time of the construction of the Great Pyramids.

The next well-documented episode of bunched collisions may have occurred a millennium later, during the period from 1350 to 1100 BCE. Here again, Baillie's evidence from tree-ring-thickness measurements shows a marked climatic downturn from 1159 to 1141 BCE, which could have been caused either directly by cometary missile impacts or by volcanoes that were triggered by such impacts.

The dates of events described in the Old Testament are open to dispute, but some at least may have occurred between 1300 and 1100 BCE. Many of the Old Testament accounts of seemingly bizarre and mysterious occurrences could have had a basis in fact if one admits the possibility of an epoch of bunched cometary impacts. Descriptions of deluges, a rain of fire on the cities of Sodom and Gomorrah, famines occasioned by the wrath of the gods—all have a rational basis as possible effects of cometary impacts. Fires, tsunamis or tidal waves, floods, climatic changes adverse to crops, even clusters of earthquakes can be interpreted as real phenomena caused by the arrival of cometary missiles. No metaphysical or mystical explanations are needed. We can also begin to understand what it was that Joshua saw when he reported that the sun stood still in the sky. It was almost certainly the glow of an immense fireball, similar to what was seen over Tunguska in June 1908. The two sets of descriptions in the Old Testament and in Siberia of 1908 are strikingly similar.

The breakup of comets during bunched collision episodes would have frequently led to spectacular displays in the ancient skies, and these in turn would have given birth to celestial combat myths in ancient societies. Such celestial combat myths involving wars of the gods are clearly found in Greek traditions, as in the Homeric poems around the eighth century BCE. It is likely that Greek mythology evolved from the older mythologies of western Asia and Mesopotamia that date back somewhat before 1100 BCE, when Earth had, indeed, suffered an episode of bombardment by cometary bolides.

A mainly benign period appears to have started a few centuries before the classical period in Greece and continued with a few remissions until the dawn of the sixth century CE. Momentous events in the sixth century CE, including the cataclysmic collapse of the Roman Empire, bear all the hallmarks of an episode of cometary missile impacts, although perhaps less intense than at earlier times. This conclusion is supported by evidence from the work of Baillie of a major downturn in Earth's climate at precisely this time. His study of tree ring thicknesses in Irish oaks shows that there was little tree growth during the years around 540 CE. Similar studies by others have also shown the same effect—narrow tree rings at this time—in places as wide afield as Germany, Scandinavia, Siberia, North America, and China. The idea that a volcanic eruption was responsible for a dust shroud that lowered the temperature and reduced seasonal tree growth does not tally with the lack of an acid signal in Greenland ice drills of the same period. Furthermore, volcanic dust is known to settle in a couple of years at most, so that cannot therefore explain such a protracted episode (535–546 CE). So there can be little doubt that a major global catastrophe enveloped the planet around the year 540 CE.

As seen from fig. 9.3 (page 85), 1,500 years from the collapse of the Roman Empire takes us forward to 2040 CE—a time that is alarmingly around the corner. If we take the sequence of events charted in fig. 9.3 seriously, we may be led to believe that the next episode of bunched collisions is imminent. However, the uncertainties are large, and the projected encounter date with our cometary debris stream could well extend beyond 2100 CE. By this time, it is to be hoped that *Homo sapiens sapiens* would have come to terms with their cosmic origins and cosmic ancestry. We may have put in place the long overdue Spaceguard project that was originally proposed by Sir Arthur C. Clarke in the

1970s. This would involve the operation of a worldwide network of small telescopes to provide advance warning of approaching comets or asteroid fragments. If and when such an offending object is found, it may be possible to use nuclear missiles or other impactors to nudge it away into a safe orbit.

CHAPTER 10

A HISTORICAL CONTEXT

I am not one who was born in the possession of knowledge;
I am one who is fond of antiquity, and earnest in seeking
it there.

CONFUCIUS (551–479 BCE)

We have seen earlier that the history of Western civilization was punctuated by the dominance of a long succession of empires. The cohesive force that held each empire together was mainly a shared identity of cultural heritage. In antiquity in the Western hemisphere, the longest running empire was that of Egypt—the Egypt of the pharaohs. A series of pharaonic dynasties ruled Egypt, producing empires that remained remarkably stable over thousands of years. The pharaohs claimed divine descent, often from Atum, the sun god. The priesthood was also important as an intermediary for administering the pharaoh's divine authority. We now know that the Egyptian civilization reached its summit with the building of the Giza pyramids around 2500 BCE. After nearly three millennia of unchallenged dominance, the throne of the pharaohs was eventually transferred to the Persian king Cambyses II in the Battle of Pelusium in 525 BCE and the Persian Empire began. Eventually, Persia came under the dominance of Greece, and much later Greece in its turn was defeated by Rome.

We have already mentioned that in relation to the main topics discussed in this book, it is to Greece during the period from the sixth to the third century BCE that we must turn. It is a remarkable fact that over a relatively small area in the Mediterranean region of our planet we witness the most remarkable flowering of the human spirit, taking place over a very short timescale. In the fifth century BCE, we see the sudden burgeoning of philosophy, poetry, drama, mathematics, and science. The classical period of Greek culture and Greek superiority begins.

It is, of course, difficult to discover unambiguously whether any connection may have existed between the ideas of the Greeks in the fifth century BCE and earlier ideas that had prevailed both in Egypt and farther east in India. Such connections have rarely been explored, but links there must surely have been. It is probably no coincidence that the time of Socrates in Greece in the fifth century BCE coincided with that of the Buddha in India and that they both used the dialectical approach in their attempts to arrive at objective truths about the world; namely, reaching the truth by pure dialogue and inquiry. It also appears likely that the Greeks in this period were rediscovering much earlier knowledge that already existed in Egypt and Babylonia. Indeed, the Greek mathematician Pythagoras is said to have traveled to both these places, according to some accounts.

In the Western world the first explicit reference to panspermia—the concept that the seeds of life are inherent in the universe—is to be found in the works of Anaxoragas (510–428 BCE). The accomplishments of Anaxoragas in astronomy were second to none and included his proposition that the sun and moon were material objects, not gods. For this heresy Anaxoragas was banished from Athens—one of the most severe punishments a citizen could receive.

Anaxoragas's views were sharply opposed by the later philosopher Aristotle (384–322 BCE), who was a pupil of Plato (428–348 BCE). Both Plato and Socrates (470–399 BCE) followed the dialectical method of philosophy. Aristotle is regarded as the innovator of the empirical method of science, the method of observing the world with experiments. This method was probably introduced to Aristotle by his father, who was a doctor and the personal physician to the king of Macedon. Aristotle continued in the tradition of dissecting animals and recording observations of nature and so developed a theory of biology in his treatise *Historia animalium*. His work was ostensibly grounded in systematic observation, which, as we have seen, sometimes turned out to be superficial and erroneous.

Aristotle remained a towering figure throughout the classical and postclassical periods in Greece, and his influence has continued into modern times. It is important to note that Aristotle's views also dominated theological thinking and scholarship in Europe in medieval times. The Aristotelean concept of a Prime Mover or First Cause was taken up by Saint Thomas Aquinas (1225–1274 CE) and interpreted by him to be the justification of a Judeo-Christian God. Likewise, Aristotle's *Metaphysics* was embraced by Muslim scholars and given pride of place in the Islamic canon.

Against this backdrop of reverence and adulation that surrounded him, two important Aristotelean principles relating to cosmology came to be cast in stone. The first was the proposition that Earth was the center of the universe, with stars, planets, and all heavenly bodies revolving in spheres around a central Earth. The second was that life of every kind arose and continues to arise spontaneously from nonliving inanimate matter on Earth. Both these assertions have turned out to be woefully wrong. But because of Aristotle's enormous stature as a philosopher, they were both adamantly held and fiercely defended, thus setting back the progress of science for centuries.

The most famous challenge of Aristotelean spontaneous generation came from the work of the French biologist Louis Pasteur in 1859. From Pasteur's famous experiments on the fermentation of wine and the souring of milk, he had demonstrated that life is always produced by life that existed before, leading to his dictum *Omne vivum ex vivo*—"all life from life." Pasteur was showered with honors and decorations for this remarkable breakthrough, but that did not change the tide of history.

A later generation of scientists, including Aleksandr Oparin, J. B. S. Haldane, and Stanley Miller in the twentieth century, began to develop their theory of the primordial soup, thus pushing back the elusive event of spontaneous generation to a remote, perhaps unknowable geological past. Despite a paucity of supportive evidence and facts and a growing body of contrary evidence, the Aristotelean idea of spontaneous generation still continues to dominate science and to cripple its progress. Pasteur's life-from-life dictum is clearly seen to be valid throughout the entire history of Earth all the way to the time before Earth itself had formed. Logic thus drives us to assert that life could not have started on Earth, so Aristotle's principle is falsified.

We have discussed in other chapters how a powerful body of evidence that proves beyond a shadow of doubt our cosmic origins is so steadfastly resisted and opposed. How this can happen in our modern rational world that is ruled by science and technology is at first sight difficult to understand. Yet ironically, the modern technologies that define our society can themselves contribute to this state of affairs. An ideology that is long past its sell-by date could be forced to maintain its supremacy by the power of social media. Dominant and powerful groups with vested interests can disseminate false propaganda at lightning speed against any rival group to the point that widespread belief in a faulty ideology becomes inevitable. This would make progress and convergence to the truth virtually impossible.

Once Aristotle had acquired a hallowed status in both Judeo-Christian and Islamic traditions, the entire canon of Aristotelean philosophy became immovable in Western culture. Aristotle's principles were taken as axioms, rather like the axioms of Euclidean geometry, so no deeper inquiry was considered either relevant or appropriate. It is no surprise, therefore, that resistance to change in regard to spontaneous generation came to be so firmly established.

Although it is difficult for us to assert with absolute certainly, in our opinion there is an unmistakable component of imperialism and racial superiority that has tainted the reception of the theory of cosmic life, which entails the abandonment of the long-cherished principle of spontaneous generation. The theory of cosmic life, which itself has an oriental provenance, was proposed in 1981 by Fred Hoyle (1915–2001) and one of us (CW) who has unmistakable oriental roots. As we have already mentioned, despite an avalanche of supportive facts and data, these ideas have been successfully disparaged and effectively kept at bay for a long time. Signs of a change of attitude are, however, clearly visible at the present time, thus fulfilling the doctrine that facts always win over prejudice in the long run.

Assertion of cultural superiority in regard to the acceptance of new facts is by no means a new phenomenon. One striking event in relatively recent history relates to the accidental discovery in 1799 of the Rosetta stone (see figure 10.1 on page 98) by French soldiers who were excavating the foundations of an ancient fort in Egypt. The stone remained in French possession until in a battle between Napoleon's forces and British soldiers resulting in a French surrender in 1801 the stone passed into British possession. The Rosetta stone contained text in two languages—Egyptian hieroglyphic and Greek—and it was carved in 196 BCE. Egyptian hieroglyphic writing, which had already been found in very many Egyptian monuments, had remained undeciphered for thousands of years. The juxtaposition of the two scripts on the Rosetta stone provided the key for its eventual deciphering and translation by French scholar Jean-Francois Champollion in 1822. From this time on scholars were able to decipher and translate for the first time vast amounts of Egyptian text, which revealed a highly sophisticated literature and level of scholarship, dating back to well before biblical times. This literature, belonging as it did to a pre-European civilization older than 1000 BCE, caused great consternation in the West. The immediate reaction of Western scholars was to declare that this was evidence of an ancient civilization but one that was necessarily far less sophisticated than that of Western Europe. When finally it had to be conceded that here was a civilization distinctly superior and more advanced than that of the West, a different response emerged. Now disbelief of the facts was tainted with unmistakable racism. Hints that the ancient Egyptians

*Fig. 10.1. The Rosetta stone, discovered in 1799,
enabled the unlocking of the legacy of ancient Egypt.
(Photo by Hans Hillewaert)*

were of African or Negro descent emerged quite early, and they were dismissed with the pronouncement that this was impossible. Egyptians, of course, had been considered to be Caucasians!

Recently clay tablets containing cuneiform texts dating back to 350 BCE were examined by Mathieu Ossendrijver of Humboldt University in Berlin and discovered to contain inscriptions showing the use of calculus. A form of calculus (hitherto thought to have been invented by Newton and Leibniz in the sixteenth century CE) was being used by the Babylonians to calculate movements of the planet Jupiter. Earlier Babylonian texts going as far back as 1800 BCE had also shown clear evidence of knowledge of algebra and geometry. The Babylonians had developed methods of solving quadratic equations and also some cubic equations millennia before the period of Classical Greece. So it is now impossible, based on these facts, to claim pure European descent of all the important ideas of mathematics, science, and philosophy.

We have so far confined attention to Mediterranean civilizations, with particular reference to those of Greece, Egypt, and Babylon. There is no doubt that developments of comparable or even greater importance were taking place farther east, in India and China. The earliest cultures in India apparently emerged in the Indus River valley around 3000 BCE. The Indus valley settlements of Harrapa and Mohenjo-daro, with their impressive archaeological ruins, provide evidence of a technologically advanced civilization that was in every way comparable or perhaps even superior to its Babylonian and Egyptian counterparts. Well-planned towns and cities endowed with wide roads, drainage systems, and buildings constructed from bricks and mortar bear testimony to a highly advanced civilization. Excavations also provided evidence that the construction of the buildings involved sophisticated surveying techniques, and it could also be inferred that they used a decimal system of counting. Mathematical knowledge in India was thus well advanced at the time.

The Indus valley civilization fell into sudden decline around

1500 BCE, and we have earlier suggested that this may have been caused by the impact of cometary bolides. The fully historical epoch in Indian history begins with the Pradyota dynasty (ca. 779–544 BCE). Thereafter a succession of dynasties takes control of the subcontinent until we arrive in the sixth century BCE. Almost at the same time Gautama Siddharth established Buddhism in India and Confucius founded Confucianism in China. Two centuries later we have King Asoka ruling over most of the subcontinent and leading an empire not by force but by the compelling power of Buddhist ideas. Asoka succeeds in spreading Buddhism to Sri Lanka, Burma, Thailand, and Cambodia, and it later reaches China and Japan. The doctrines of compassion and universal life take root over a large part of the Orient.

To conclude this chapter we return to the history and prehistory of panspermia. It was already mentioned that Buddhist texts make clear reference to the multiplicity of inhabited planets, with direct implications for panspermia. Even earlier Vedic texts leave little doubt as to the widespread prevalence of the living worlds and of life being a truly cosmic phenomenon. Recently Robert Temple has pointed out that the antecedents of the panspermia theory go back in ancient Egypt to the Old Kingdom in the third millennium BCE. This was a time when Egyptian civilization had reached its highest peak, and it is, indeed, remarkable to find that ideas of panspermia and cosmic life are so explicitly displayed. The Egyptian texts and depictions suggest that the whole cosmos is full of seeds and that life on Earth originated from them. Panspermia then appears to be as old as civilization itself (Temple 2007).

CHAPTER 11

SO WHAT IF WE CAME FROM SPACE?

*If you can look into the seeds of time, and say which grain
will grow and which will not, speak then to me.*
WILLIAM SHAKESPEARE, *MACBETH*, ACT 1:3

The cynic might well ask, So what if we came from space? What is all the fuss about? As we have mentioned already, the implications of accepting this fact are profound. The new paradigm would have a direct bearing on the entire future of humanity; it would transform science, philosophy, religion, and civilization itself. The grand cosmic-centered worldview that embraces biology will force a total rewrite of the history of life on our planet. It would also guide us on the path to devising new rules for preserving the fast-diminishing resources of Earth and new rules of conduct for survival.

Nothing of any innovative significance ever happened on Earth. Our planet Earth was merely an assembly site, one of trillions in the universe, on which preordered genetic structures (viruses) came together to be assembled into the multitude of life-forms we see on Earth today. This knowledge could (or should) make us more respectful of all life and more vigilant in preserving and protecting the species that we have

101

on Earth, some of which on the verge of extinction. It could (or should) strengthen the bonds of kinship that unite diverse races, creeds, and faith groups on our planet. In 2019 the world is embroiled in many bitter conflicts. Political ideologies, races, castes, and subcastes are at loggerheads in many parts of the world. No difference can be too small to generate disharmony and conflict.

The new worldview that beckons should have the effect of preserving the unity of all people on the planet, respecting the fact that we are all creatures of the cosmos. All religions will also merge into one universal truth when logic eventually prevails. Religion will imply the acceptance of a cosmic intelligence to which we all owe allegiance. This point of view will replace the multiplicity of faiths, gods, and rituals that is the cause of the dissension and conflict we see at the present time. This might be easier said than done. Religious institutions that have become so well established over the centuries and millennia will resist change, at least for a while. But when they see that the traditional theological views are metaphors for a much grander cosmic reality, they will be swayed.

There will undoubtedly be logistic difficulties in regard to continuing programs of scientific research. The accommodation of major scientific projects that are now in progress within a new framework will also pose difficulties, but we hope they could be overcome. For instance, expensive space programs directed at looking for independent origins of life on other planets should be abandoned. Instead, we will have to intensify our search for life on other planetary bodies, including distant exoplanets. The search for intelligent life elsewhere in the universe will also acquire a new sense of urgency. Cosmic life must logically imply a convergence to intelligence occurring everywhere. Projects such as SETI that were relegated to the status of low priority in the past few decades would soar in importance. This will be particularly important if positive signals are detected from nearby exoplanets in the foreseeable future.

When our cosmic origins are understood and conceded, it will also become clear that bacteria and viruses coming to Earth from outside could sometimes pose serious threats of pandemic disease, not only to humans but also to plants and animals. This is connected with an idea that was explored as early as 1979—that most of the pandemics throughout history were, indeed, driven from space with the arrival of new viruses and bacteria. With all the data that is currently available across a wide spectrum of disciplines, we believe there is an urgent need for the possibility of bacterial and viral ingress from space to be taken seriously.

If hard scientific facts were all that really matter, our cosmic genetic ancestry and everything that follows from it would be considered as self-evident. However, as we saw in earlier chapters, concerted attempts to deny this are being made, and they are all connected more with sociology than science. Such considerations are far removed from a proper assessment of fact and have more to do with human failings—pride, self-esteem, arrogance, greed, and envy! People whose entire scientific careers were devoted to arguing for geocentric biology will not be able to switch their thinking easily. And because such individuals tend to be politically powerful, their views will prevail for a while.

By the very nature of things, however, the days are numbered for all those who hold wrong views. A new generation is on the way, and they would find it advantageous to change the old order. Stripped bare of all the prejudices of earlier generations, they will realize that accepting the simple and elegant tenet of cosmic life instantly gives them new opportunities. New vistas of science would be opened that it would be their privilege to explore.

For the average citizen the realization that our basic genetic makeup owes its origin to the external universe is a big enough shock to start with. Then they are told that the ensemble of viruses that made them was actually put together by a supremely intelligent cosmic entity inherent in the structure of the universe. For those of us with prior religious convictions this latter step may come as a profound shock. The old theistic connection states

$$God \rightarrow Man \rightarrow God$$

This is far too simple, and this is better replaced with

$$Universe \rightarrow Cosmic\ Intelligence \rightarrow \ ..... \rightarrow Man \rightarrow Universe.$$

It's a big jump, indeed, but in our view inevitable.

The arrows in the first equation refer to an undefined process, whereas the arrows in the second refer to the transfer of coded information in the form of viral genes. We have touched on the topic of consciousness in earlier chapters, pointing to a possible link between consciousness and higher dimensions in modern descriptions of the quantum universe. Again, the emerging trend, we believe, will be to regard conscious living beings as entities that are intimately and inextricably connected to the logical structure of the cosmos at the deepest level.

It has been mentioned by several commentators that ideas of consciousness, which are still admittedly very hazy, might lie at the interface between quantum mechanics and classical physics. According to Roger Penrose and others, the inadequacies of our present theories of quantum physics are likely to be the reason our knowledge on these matters is, indeed, so hazy. In any case, we can conclude with reasonable confidence that if life is a cosmic phenomenon, so also must consciousness be understood on the same terms. Consciousness that is manifest even in the humblest ant or bee must be seen as an emergent property of an inherently intelligent universe, not an accidental by-product of evolution confined to Earth.

Our own preference is therefore for the logical sequence:

$$Universe \rightarrow Cosmic\ Intelligence \rightarrow Man \rightarrow Universe$$

This is far superior to

$$God \rightarrow Man \rightarrow God$$

We have to concede that the ideas that follow from an acceptance of our cosmic origins show an immediate preference for the Vedic-Buddhist canon of ideas. Whether Judeo-Christian traditions that dominate the modern Western world today will adapt to accommodate these ideas remains to be seen.

In the modern twenty-first century world, we have witnessed an alarming escalation of international belligerence and a consequent expansion of nuclear weaponry. The totality of global nuclear arsenals today probably has the capacity to exterminate all humans on Earth, perhaps even all life. Although one hopes that sanity will eventually prevail and that the lessons of Hiroshima and Nagasaki will have been learned, the present situation is admittedly highly unstable and to a large extent unpredictable.

On the hundreds of billions of other Earth-like planets that most probably exist in the galaxy, the same viruses that led to life on Earth, including humans, would have rained in the past, would be still raining, or would do so in the future. By a process of convergent evolution, we would expect parallel developments of intelligent life to emerge elsewhere. On those planets where the realization of cosmic origins had dawned, we might expect self-preserving philosophies, perhaps similar to Buddhism, to have also arisen. Other alien cosmic civilizations that turned a blind eye to their cosmic origins (as we unfortunately do today) would pursue a path toward self-destruction. Thus, through a process of natural selection, it will be the civilizations that accepted their cosmic ancestry that will survive and dominate in number.

In conclusion, we reiterate the importance of acknowledging our cosmic origins without delay. This acceptance will require major readjustments of our thinking and our perception of who we are. It will mark the beginning of a revolution more profound and far-reaching than any we have witnessed before. Over thousands of years our perception of who we are and how we relate to the external world has changed. Starting from the smallest group to which loyalty is owed—the nuclear family—we have expanded to the extended family, then to the small tribe, to the city-state, the nation-state, to all humanity, and eventually to all life that shares our biosphere.

The next transition must be to the full recognition that we are part of a vast, perhaps infinite, living system. This in turn will lead to the establishment of new rules for survival and for the preservation of our environment.

CHAPTER 12

THE WORLD OF 2100

Study the past if you would divine the future.

CONFUCIUS (551–479 BCE)

This Confucian dictum cannot be easily challenged. Extrapolating from the present and recent past into a future that is unknown is not without its risks. Certain trends, however, are discernible over decades, centuries, and millennia, and they can be extrapolated with varying degrees of certainty and confidence.

In 1945 Arthur C. Clarke, the doyen of science fiction and a visionary, published a paper in *Wireless World* proposing the case for a geostationary satellite that could connect the entire planet in a global communication network. A satellite in a circular orbit at Earth's equator at a particular distance of 42,164 kilometers from the center of Earth has a period of revolution exactly equal to Earth's rotation on its axis and would remain geostationary over the same point on Earth's equator. The first communication satellite was launched into the so-called "Clarke orbit" in 1961; in 2017 the total tally was 401. It is this technology that has given rise to all the aspects of life in 2019 that we take for granted. Instant worldwide communication and the internet are part and parcel of modern life. It is worth reflecting on how dramatically our lives have been changed by Clarke's prediction, accompanied, of course, by the rapid explosion of computer and information technology. In 1964 Clarke made the following statement at the 1964 World's Fair in New York:

> Predicting the future is hazardous occupation because the prophet invariably falls between two stools. If his predictions are at all reasonable you can predict in twenty or at least fifty years that the progress of science and technology would make him seem ridiculously conservative. On the other hand if, by some miracle, a prophet could describe the future exactly as it was going to take place, his prediction will sound so absurd, so far-fetched, that everybody would laugh him to scorn. This has proved to be true in the past and it will undoubtedly be true even more so in the century to come. The only thing we can be sure of the future is that it will be absolutely fantastic.

Fig. 12.1. N. Chandra Wickramasinghe with Arthur C. Clarke in his study in Colombo, Sri Lanka, 1984

In Clarke's book *Greetings, Carbon-Based Bipeds!: Collected Essays 1934–1998,* he makes several bold predictions of the future, some of which have already come true. Others lie in wait.

- By **2010** commercial nuclear devices, household quantum generators, and fully reengineered automobile engines will have ended the fossil fuel age. We'll have seen the first acknowledged human clone and seen off the last human criminal.

- By **2020** we'll have discovered a seventy-six-meter octopus, will fly on "aerospace-planes," and will trade in "mega-watt-hours" instead of any now-known currencies. Tsunamis caused by a meteor strike will have wrecked the coasts of Greenland and Canada (prompting the development of new meteor-detecting technologies).

- By **2030** artificial intelligence will have reached a human level, we'll have landed on Mars, computer-generated DNA will make possible a real-life Jurassic Park, and the neurological "braincap" will allow us the direct sensory experience of anything at all.

- By **2040** the "universal replicator" will allow us to create any object at all in the comfort of our own homes, resulting in the phase-out of work and a boom in arts, entertainment, and education.

- By **2050** Buckminster Fuller–style self-contained mobile homes will have become a reality, and humans scattered as far as "Earth, the Moon, Mars, Europa, Ganymede, and Titan and in orbit around Venus, Neptune, and Pluto" will celebrate the centenary of Sputnik 1.

- By **2090** Halley's comet will have returned, and on it we'll have found life-forms that vindicate "Wickramasinghe and Hoyle's century-old hypothesis that life exists through space." We'll also start burning fossil fuels again, both as a replacement for the carbon dioxide we've "mined" from the air and to forestall the next ice age by warming the globe back up a bit.

- By **2100** we'll have replaced rockets with a "space drive" that lets us travel close to the speed of light.

It is noteworthy that we're already somewhat behind Clarke's vision, according to which in 2010 and even 2019 many a still-improbable development lies in the near future. One of us (CW) was a friend of Clarke and enjoyed many exhilarating discussions. He was a great supporter of the idea of cosmic life and wrote the following in a foreword to the 2001 book (by CW) *Cosmic Dragons: Life and Death on Our Planet:*

> Bohr is reported to have said to a fellow scientist "We all agree that your theory is crazy —but we don't think it's crazy enough to be true." Well, I think Chandra's theory *is* crazy enough to be true, and I am more and more convinced now that life has spread throughout the universe probably by the very mechanism he proposes. (Wickramasinghe 2001)

Such an endorsement by a great prophet of futurism is faint praise, indeed. His later prediction that a total vindication of cosmic life by 2090 would take place at the next approach of Halley's comet might sound unduly pessimistic. In this instance he has miscalculated by perhaps seventy years!

The year 2100, the dawn of the next century, is regarded as a benchmark date for projecting and predicting human progress. There is scarcely any doubt that this new century will herald an "absolutely fantastic" world in the sense that Clarke suggests. It will be a future totally beyond our comprehension. Just as some of our parents or grandparents have sometimes gasped in utter bewilderment at our modern world, so would we if we were transported by a time machine into the world of 2100.

In the run-up to 2100, perhaps long before, will come the ungrudging acceptance of our cosmic origins. This will signify a societal enlightenment on a global scale not unlike the enlightenment experienced by the Buddha in the fifth century BCE. The Buddha's iconic smile of contentment and expression of inner peace will, we hope, dawn on the entire world. The world of the twentieth century, a world riven by wars and strife between nations, races, clans, and religions, will have long since disappeared. Freed from the shackles of a false hypothesis, our bounds of kinship and sympathy will extend to include all human beings, all living things, and even all life in the universe. War and the fear of war will have all but vanished.

In 2016 the total world military expenditure was estimated to have been $1,686 billion, equivalent to 2.2 percent of the global gross domestic product (GDP); see figure 12.2 (page 112). This amounts to about $227 per individual, and although it might sound like a small amount, this money, if suitably used, would have the potential to alleviate global poverty to a noticeable degree.

The military technologies that were developed throughout the twentieth century may not be entirely wasted if they can be deployed in a positive way. One possible use is connected with attacking—diverting and fragmenting—incoming cosmic missiles before they hit Earth. This would require advanced telescopic detection of a potentially threatening object and then diverting it using nuclear missiles.

After the monumental task of sequencing the entire human genome was achieved in 2001, manipulation of genomes, including the human genome, has been carried out to a variety of ends. Human genome technology is now available that can delete a mutant gene responsible for

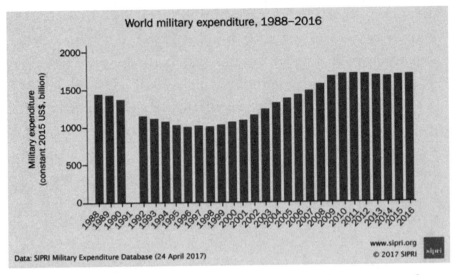

Fig. 12.2. World military expenditure, year by year (Data courtesy of Stockholm International Peace Research Institute military expenditure database, April 24, 2017, © 2017 SIPRI)

a disease and insert a healthy one. By 2100 this technique will have advanced to the stage that almost all genetically based human diseases will be banished. It is in this way that we project an average human life span to increase to 150 years by the turn of the next century.

Until recently, gene manipulation techniques were deployed only on embryos of laboratory animals, ethical consideration barring their use in humans. The fear that such genetic engineering will lead to a quest for producing designer babies or even a superrace itself continues to haunt us. By the middle of the present century, we believe that these fears will have given way to a pragmatic acceptance of the benefits of the new technology. In the context of what we have discussed in chapter 6, it is possible that by 2100 we will have isolated the alien (cosmic) genes that we categorized as Le and Lu and perhaps could manipulate them to our collective advantage. Take on the good and reject the bad.

It is likely that genomic modification of humans, and even other animals, may have progressed far beyond what we can even imagine today. For instance, the mode of acquisition of information and scientific knowledge may have been transformed beyond our wildest dreams by developments in the science of information technology combined with advances in neuroscience. Acquiring technical expertise may not require attendance of courses at university or twentieth-century-style tutorials, but rather plug-in modules that link directly into our brains. "Fantastic," as Clarke described it, but entirely possible from the rate of progress we witness today. Whether Clarke's prediction that other animals—for example, monkeys—will be genetically engineered to be our servants, performing the more menial tasks like those of hotel doormen, comes to fruition remains to be seen. If this were to happen, we would see a return to slavery of a new kind.

Space exploration, which had proceeded with unstoppable speed from the dawn of the space age in the 1960s, would have long ago come to a dead end. By the year 2030 the exorbitant space projects that were disingenuously designed to search for origins of life on other planetary bodies in the solar system—Jupiter's moon Europa, for instance—may have been deemed a waste of money and duly scrapped. It is amazing, in retrospect, that we could have been collectively so stupid as to think that the solar system, with its many exchanges of material between different bodies, is not one single connected biosphere. Life on Earth surely implies life everywhere across the solar system, the only condition being that of survival.

In 2100 our space eyes may be fixed on our nearest exoplanets. The first such planet outside our solar system was discovered in 1995, and by 2017 some three thousand definite detections of exoplanets had been made, most of them being discovered by NASA's orbiting Kepler satellite in a minute sampling volume of the Milky Way. Such detections are made by measuring the minute dips in the brightness of stars as planets transit in front of them and block out a fraction of starlight. The total projected tally of such exoplanets in the galaxy now runs into some 140 billion, one for every sunlike star. The nearest exoplanet to us is an Earth-sized planet around the star Proxima Centauri at a distance of 3.1 light years—literally in our cosmic backyard!

At every stage in human history we believed that we had the ultimate knowledge of the nature of the cosmos, how big it is, and how it originated. Every such model in the past turned out to be wrong. In 2019 the entire scientific establishment has rallied around one particular model—the standard hot big bang cosmology. It started off as an elegant, simple idea, first proposed in 1927 by the Belgian Catholic priest Georges Lemaître, in which the universe is posited to have started ex nihilo from a gigantic explosion—the big bang. One cannot but notice that this scientific idea looks like an almost perfect rendering of the biblical story of creation. The First Cause or Prime Mover would appear to be concealed in the big bang itself. The theory received almost instant support after Edwin Hubble discovered that galaxies are moving away from each other at speeds proportional to their distance. Einstein's new theories of space and time combined with Hubble's data gave instant approbation for the big bang cosmology, and this then became over the subsequent years the standard model of the universe.

Although the big bang model was challenged by Fred Hoyle, Hermann Bondi, and Thomas Gold in the 1950s and 1960s, these challenges were eventually fenced off, and various versions of Lamaître's big bang cosmology remain the favored model in 2019, the so-called standard cosmological model. With a flurry of new observations of the most distant galaxies, cracks are surfacing in this popular cosmological model. The model requires the presence of dark nonluminous matter to explain how stars in galaxies rotate around a central axis. The identity of this dark matter is still a matter for speculation, and no final answer is available at the present time.

Even by our target year of 2100, we do not think this matter will have been resolved. The oscillating cosmological models supported by Neil Turok at the University of Cambridge suggest that the apparent big bang represents just one stage in an infinite sequence of expansion and contraction—big bangs followed by big crunches. In this model neither the universe nor time have a definite beginning or end. This is amazingly consistent with the Hindu and Buddhist views of the universe.

The world of subatomic physics will also come to be transformed beyond recognition by the dawn of the next century. We knew in 2019 that matter is composed of atoms, which in turn are made of electrons and a central nucleus. The nucleus in its turn is made of neutrons and protons. Electrons are a class of independent fundamental particles known as leptons. Other leptons are known by the names muons, tauons, and three separate neutrinos. The neutrons and protons, on the other hand, are made of smaller units known as quarks. Quarks come in several forms—up, down, charm, strange, bottom, and top. A proton is made of two up quarks and one down quark. A neutron is made up of two down quarks and one up quark. The standard model of particle physics includes a description of these fundamental building blocks as well as the forces by which they interact. Although the description of this quantum world is close to complete, the interface between the quantum world and the classical world described by Newton and Einstein still remains elusive. It is in this interface that the description of consciousness would appear to lurk—perhaps to be elucidated by 2010, perhaps not.

What will have developed beyond all expectation by this time is the science of materials—materials that can make things from nuts and bolts to buildings. New forms of carbon known as graphene and biologically generated plastics will have replaced conventional bricks, mortar, steel, and concrete, with the advantage that such materials are produced with great efficiency and with minimal cost to the environment.

The human population in 2100 will by present trends have risen to eleven billion and will require intensive use of available land resources to provide housing. It might be inevitable to use areas of the planet now covered with forest, desert, or even ice, for human habitation.

Skyscrapers similar to those in New York or Dubai will be everywhere to be seen. It may even be necessary to have people in "artificial cities" floating in the oceans.

Global poverty, which was the scourge of the twentieth and twenty-first centuries, will have been greatly alleviated by new economic and agricultural strategies. With a tightly enforced control of world population, the challenge will be to produce enough food to maintain the population at an acceptable level of subsistence. This will demand new and more efficient agricultural methods that require minimal energy and have less environmental impact compared with conventional farming. It has been known for some time that our protein nutritional requirements can, if we so desire, be met from protein derived from microbiological sources—bacteria and algae. However, in the early decades of the twenty-first century, such protein was used mainly for livestock and fish food within the framework of conventional agriculture.

Well before 2100 it will have been recognized that microbial protein provides a balanced alternative to fish and meat in our diet and that its production in sunlit transparent domes is extremely economical, both in space and on our planetary resources. The twenty-second century may well be said to be the century of vegans: all our food will eventually be produced from microbial sources. The cosmic microbes from which we evolved in the first place would provide all our food to survive.

It is almost certain that the technological race to provide more efficient modes of transport in the form of cars, trains, ships, and airplanes will have reached its natural end. With an ultrafast and efficient internet, most people will be conducting all their business from home. Recreational facilities will be within walking distance of where people live. In these circumstances travel will only be for recreation, and such travel may well include travel to other solar system planetary bodies.

Our economic and monetary system in 2019 is riddled with complexity often linked to treaties and agreements between nations. The major factor that controls wealth is tied to the supply of petroleum, the main producers of which are Russia, Saudi Arabia, the United States, and Iraq. The struggle to appropriate and control this oil wealth is the root of most of the conflicts in the modern world.

It has been recognized throughout the twentieth century that our profligacy in the use of our limited planetary reserves of fossil fuels (oil and coal) comes with a heavy burden. Besides international conflicts and wars, the burning of fossil fuels leads to environmental degradation, as seen, for instance, in the cities of modern China. Furthermore, the amount of available fossil fuels, although unknown, is not unlimited. So it is prudent to look for alternative sources of energy if industrial progress is to continue at an acceptable pace.

An alternative energy source that is used extensively in the twenty-first century is nuclear—nuclear fission. This involves harnessing the energy locked in the nuclei of atoms, in particular the radioactive element uranium. Over a few decades, this has proved to be a relatively inexpensive way of producing electricity, but again, the available deposits of uranium are limited and would not last even a century at the present rate of its use. The familiar downside of the fission of uranium is, of course, the disposal of radioactive waste. This is a problem that has not yet been solved. We have already discussed this problem in chapter 6.

Of all the renewable energy sources that have been explored in the twentieth and twenty-first centuries, the direct use of solar energy promises to offer the best hope for the future. The sun shines by the fusion of hydrogen to helium, which takes place under the high temperatures and pressures that prevail in its interior. This is a cost-free energy source that will be available for at least the next two billion years. All life on Earth has actually used this energy source for billions of years in the past. What remains for humans to do is to collect this energy using the next generation solar panels made up of packages of superefficient photovoltaic cells. In this way sunlight is converted and stored as electricity. Developments in producing increasingly efficient solar panels would ensure that the energy requirements of the eleven billion humans in 2100 could be met entirely by using solar energy.

The world order, after our cosmic origins are unreservedly conceded, would be drastically different from what we recognize today. In 2019 our home planet Earth, with its seven-billion-member population distributed into some 195 nation-states, is a world of enormous inequality and contrast. The distribution of power, wealth, and resources varies hugely. The per capita income of the richest nation, Qatar, is some $141,000, compared with $250 for the poorest nation, Malawi, a disparity by a factor of more than five hundred; the factor compared with the United States is 228. In 2017 the countries commanding world influence were ranked in the order of (1) United States, (2) Russia, and (3) China.

In 2019, after a century of two devastating world wars, an uneasy peace prevails. Several potential conflicts are held at bay, but perhaps only just. The last nuclear attack, on Nagasaki and Hiroshima in 1945, is now a distant memory. Despite the many warnings that have been uttered by experts against nuclear arms proliferation, the development of even more deadly nuclear weapons still continues. We, or at least our politicians, have not learned any lessons from the past.

Our modern desire to maintain independent nations is deeply rooted in history and may well be even a relic of our distant tribal past. When our ancestors lived in small tribes, their survival depended on holding fast to the patch of land they had appropriated and cultivated for growing food. Tribal boundaries would then have been rigorously maintained and defended against intruders from other tribes. Tribes would also develop their own customs and rituals that would serve as expressions of group identity, thus distinguishing one tribe from another. Modern nation-states are often (though not always) separated by race, religion, history, and language. Fear of invasion and attack by other states has in the past provided an important incentive for preserving national unity. In the world of the future, these fears will become irrelevant. Societal cohesion is now to be sought—pledging loyalty to the whole of humanity as well as all life on Earth and in the wider cosmos.

This is the utopia that beckons.

THE NEW COSMIC WORLDVIEW

The new cosmic worldview that is now essentially proven by rigorous science holds out great promise and an equal measure of sacrifice. The promise is of true knowledge unimpeded by cultural bias, enlightenment, and a life that will be in complete harmony with nature—Earth and the universe. Idealistic as it may sound, this will, indeed, be the logical outcome that follows. We could expect the world of the future to be for the most part free of racial, economic, territorial, religious, or intergenerational strife, and as individuals we should enjoy a happy and contented life.

The sacrifice we face will be a diminution of our sense of self-importance and pride. We would recognize that *Homo sapiens sapiens* is on the cosmic scale neither unique nor supreme. For centuries we have deceived ourselves in believing that we are the most important life-form in the universe. We have also prided ourselves as being supremely intelligent and powerful. It is amply clear that on the road to the development of intelligence we are very much at the beginning, not the end. With higher levels of intelligence and the realization of a sense of cosmic consciousness, we would be living in closer harmony with nature; we would also be expending less energy and achieving more. Let us hope we can free ourselves from the chains of nonsolar (nuclear) energy slavery and develop technologies to depend solely on the exploitation of solar energy.

What steps must we take to realize such goals? First and foremost, we must find ways to stop our present wasteful spending on weapons of war and to a lesser extent on showboat science that has little or no value. The most expensive space projects currently in progress, which involve the search for life on distant planets, must be abandoned. We know for sure that there exists life on every planet or object in the universe where it could survive. Carbon in complex molecules and polymer chains is seen everywhere, and all this must come from life. The quest for a prebiotic chemistry must be scrapped. The only scientific rule worth respecting is that life always produces more life. This was known from the work of Louis Pasteur in the nineteenth century, but such a profound truth about the world was not convenient for scientists of the day. The patterns of evolution we witness on Earth must also be universal; the same genetic components are involved everywhere. The emergence of intelligence must be regarded as commonplace, and the longest-lived intelligence in the universe would surely belong to those who acknowledged their cosmic origins and consequently adopted a philosophy of peaceful coexistence with the planet, which we may call "an etiquette of living on Earth."

After the divergent ideas about religion and God that prevailed in the twentieth century have given way to the new cosmic worldview, religious strife will end. Conflicts between nations will also be reduced once the mad scramble to grab the planet's nonrenewable energy resources becomes progressively less important. New and cleaner sources of energy will be sought, discovered, and harnessed. New scientific research will also seek to make the next generation of machines and devices far less energy intensive than they are today.

In the twentieth and early twenty-first centuries, the world was divided into many warring nation-states, each striving to achieve dominance and supremacy. Large armies and military power were needed for this purpose. The distinguishing criteria of twenty-first-century nationhood included a complex mix of shared history, political philosophy, religion, and sometimes ethnicity or race. Such criteria effectively defined boundaries between states and nations. The desire to maintain boundaries inevitably led to war. We expect the new emerging worldview to remove the need for such national boundaries and hence eliminate the rationale for war. Let us hope that the only ideology that survives and dominates in the world beyond 2100 is that of our inalienable cosmic origins.

This raises an important question relating to our genetic inheritance and instinct. The origins of human behavior go back to the days of our most primitive cave-dwelling ancestors hundreds of thousands of years ago. They lived in harmony with nature, surviving on nature's bounty while always striving to preserve its integrity. They also lived in small tribes, and each tribe guarded its territory against invasion from neighboring tribes. Combat between neighboring tribes may have been easily triggered in a fight for survival. Our modern tendency of unlimited greed, envy, and desire to grab territory and hold onto possessions also undoubtedly goes back to these distant days. In the twentieth and twenty-first centuries our ancient combative instinct found an outlet in wars, which have become progressively more brutal and savage as the power of weapons increased. Wars of religion, at any rate wars inspired by religious beliefs, have also become a menace in recent years. We hope, with the adoption of our cosmic worldview, such wars and conflicts will become a thing of the past. Our cosmic connection will be expected to supersede all religious divisions—at any rate, that will be our hope.

When our warring instincts against one another have been tamed and excessive greed subdued, our next round of combat must be against the forces of nature. We need to face issues such as climate change, real or imagined, as well as the degradation of the environment caused by burning fossil fuels. These are matters of the utmost importance for humanity.

In our view the current obsession with studies of global warming, often uncritically attributed to anthropogenic activities, will turn out to be mistaken. Much effort has been expended on this enterprise with little or no visible sign of returns. We will soon realize that the extent of the global warming we have experienced in the last fifty years was not mainly due to human activities. Relatively warmer periods and colder periods have come and gone throughout recorded history. For instance, during the early Christian era the south of England was warm enough to grow grapes, and from 1645 to 1715 a mini–ice age gripped much of Europe. Such temperature fluctuations are part of a natural cosmic cycle unconnected with human activities.

On much longer timescales that last typically for one hundred thousand years, major glaciations—ice ages—have alternated with much briefer warm interglacial interludes that persist for an average of ten thousand years. Our present warm interglacial period is now alarmingly close to the end of its ten-thousand-year lease. So it is an imminent return to an ice age and not global warming that we should really fear and prepare for.

Human beings from the very earliest times have felt a need for intellectual challenges that go beyond mere survival in order to justify their lives. This need came into sharp focus perhaps five million years ago when, judged from the sizes of skulls of different dates, our ancestors' brains doubled in volume. This remarkable event in our evolution was almost surely brought about by the acquisition of space-borne viruses bearing new genes. A similar discontinuity in our evolution occurred not long afterward and led to the acquisition of FOXP2 genes and the consequent development of speech and communication. This event enabled us to transmit experience and evolve as social animals. It is from this point on that art, music, science, and culture began to flourish.

The earliest nonintellectual challenges our ancestors faced were most certainly concerned with basic problems of survival and establishing ever more firmly our role as the top predator of the planet. But as time went on and our basic survival was ensured, we began to explore deeper and more abstract questions not directly linked to survival. The exploration of the universe began in earnest, and the deepest questions of philosophy were asked: Why are we here? What is the purpose of life? Where did we come from? Where are we going?

From the very earliest observations of stars and planets, astronomy began to develop. At first astronomy served a purely utilitarian purpose. Knowing the positions of planets in the sky informed us of the changing seasons and told us when to sow crops and when to reap. At a slightly later stage, when our ancestors began to sail the seas, astronomy became a tool for navigation. Still later astronomy came to be intertwined with astrology and superstition.

From the middle of the fifteenth century to the present day, astronomy has developed and advanced enormously. We have now reached the stage of sending spacecraft to explore planets and comets and deploying orbiting telescopes to probe the most distant galaxies in the universe. All these endeavors are increasing steadily, and there is no end in sight. Maybe in due course physicists may arrive at their long-awaited theory of everything!

The explosion of computer science and information technology in recent years is without precedent in the entire history of human inventions. In a few decades it will probably transform our lives more profoundly than we can ever imagine. Starting off as mere aids to computation and as code-breaking accessories in the 1940s and 1950s, computers and their accompanying software have advanced enormously and invaded every nook and cranny of our modern world. As individuals, we have become utterly dependent on our smartphones, iPads, and other portable computing devices. We can't travel anywhere without being able to connect with the all-pervasive internet—a gigantic network of information and communication across the planet.

In a societal context every activity and every service you can think of—utilities, communications, administration, hospitals, education, shopping, travel—is a slave to computers and the internet. Robots have replaced humans wherever possible. There is no end to this "computerization" process in sight, and if it is used creatively and wisely, there is no end to our progress.

Increasing the efficiency of communication will not by itself lead to progress unless truth rather than falsehood is the intellectual commodity that is respected and communicated. In matters relating to our cosmic origins the unfortunate fact has been that a blatant falsehood has been unashamedly propagated using every available technology over the past few decades. Long after our cosmic ancestry has been apparent beyond a shadow of doubt, the contrary Aristotelean view of Earth-centered biology was propagated with every assistance that new technologies were able to offer. This type of abuse of a powerful new technology is most dangerous and must be condemned and eradicated.

Of course, there is no end in sight for further progress in the development of information and communication technologies. Nor, indeed, is there an end in sight for the exploration of the physical as well as the biological universe. Developments in medical science and biotechnology are also on the steepest ascent at the present time. The more we discover, the more there remains to be discovered. We have discussed some of these questions in earlier chapters.

At some point in the foreseeable future science and technology will have to focus on coping with the next ice age, which might just be around the corner. In this context we might consider ways of increasing—not decreasing—the greenhouse absorbers in the atmosphere, if this can be done without causing unacceptable levels of environmental pollution. Perhaps we could think of maintaining a cloud of orbiting iron needles to prevent long-wave (heat) radiation from escaping Earth.

Besides preparing to deal with the next ice age, it would also be prudent to prepare for a devastating pandemic that might be around the corner. In view of what we have discussed in earlier chapters, it would be wise to develop an early warning system for future pandemics. Since we now know that viruses and bacteria are constantly arriving from space, surveillance of the stratosphere will be needed to prevent a major pandemic that could possibly wipe us out entirely. This could be done, for instance, by a regular microbiological sampling of the stratosphere using balloons. As soon as a potentially dangerous pathogen—virus or bacterium—is detected, a mitigation strategy should be put in place. The descent of a virus from the stratosphere to the ground could take several months, which would give enough time for mass immunization strategies to be put in place. In this way the human species might be saved from either extinction or genetic retrogression.

Once security from pandemics has been taken care of, there remains a far more serious threat to consider—the threat of extinction from impacts of comets and asteroids. This threat is thought to be of very low probability but of very high "impact." It is difficult to estimate the precise probability of this contingency from the data that exists at the present time. As we have seen in chapter 9, many species-extinction events in the distant geological past could be attributed to comet or asteroid collisions. We know these impacts must happen, but how often we cannot be sure. One collision event that is beyond dispute is a collision with a comet that took place sixty-five million years ago and led to the extinction of the dinosaurs and, indeed, of over 85 percent of all life on Earth. New research has shown that the woolly mammoths, giant sloths, and saber-toothed tigers that roamed over the Northern Hemisphere were wiped out by a devastating comet or asteroid impact 12,900 years ago. This event may also have played a part in snapping Earth out of the last ice age.

A careful and systematic telescopic survey of the skies would be needed to spot in advance any comets and asteroids that are pursuing potentially threatening orbits. If an offending object is spotted, mitigation strategies should be put into action. From 2001 onward, scientists have been thinking about such a Spaceguard project with the deployment of a worldwide network of small telescopes dedicated to this purpose. But this has not been considered of high enough priority by the powerful nations of the world, who are still obsessed with military projects to defend themselves against each other. With our emergent new worldview, we hope sanity will dawn.

Even if we humans are clever enough to avoid both the danger of pandemics and of comet or asteroid impacts, a further threat remains. Despite all our advances in electronics, computer science, and biotechnology, a residual threat of destruction through nuclear war still looms large on the horizon. As we mentioned earlier, our combative instincts are most likely the remnants of an inherited trait that goes back to our Stone Age days. While the dawn of our new cosmic worldview should in principle eliminate the need for future combat, even a residual trace of such a tendency could lead to a potential threat of nuclear war. At the present time, the total firepower of all the nuclear arsenals of the world is perhaps enough to extinguish all life on our planet. If this is to be avoided, we think it is imperative that a cosmic and essentially Buddhist worldview prevails.

On a much longer timescale, perhaps over a few billion years into the future, our biotechnology would surely have advanced to the stage that we can pack an entire human genome, including perhaps our consciousness, into the tiniest speck of dust. Our technologies might also permit the production of vast numbers of humans and other life-forms "compressed" within dust grains that we can fling out of Earth at high enough speed to escape the solar system and reach neighboring extrasolar planetary systems.

The deadline for this final project must be before the sun enters its red giant phase and swallows up Earth. We would then have returned to where we came from.

BIBLIOGRAPHY

Arrhenius, Svante. 1908. *Worlds in the Making.* London: Harper.

Bacon, Sir Francis. 1939. *Novum organum.* In *The English Philosophers from Bacon to Mill,* edited by E. A. Burtt, 24–123. New York: Random House. Original work published in 1620.

Bailey, M. E., S. V. M. Clube, and William M. Napier. 1990. *The Origin of Comets.* Oxford: Pergamon, 72–78.

Baillie, M. G. L. 2007. "Tree-Rings Indicate Global Environmental Downturns That Could Have Been Caused by Comet Debris." In *Comet/Asteroid Impacts and Human Society: An Interdisciplinary Approach,* edited by Peter T. Bobrowsky and Hans Rickman, 105–22. Berlin: Springer-Verlag.

Barash, David. 2014. "Is Buddhism the Most Science-Friendly Religion?" *Scientific American,* February 11 (guest blog).

Boulding, Kenneth E. 1968. *Beyond Economics.* Ann Arbor: The University of Michigan Press.

Clarke, Arthur C. 1945. "V2 for Ionosphere Research?" *Wireless World,* February, 45.

———. (1999) 2010. *Greetings, Carbon-Based Bipeds!: Collected Essays 1934–1998.* London: Voyager.

Galbraith, John Kenneth. 1975. *Money.* Boston: Houghton Mifflin Company.

Georgescu-Roegen, Nicholas. 1971. *The Entropy Law and the Economic Process.* Cambridge, Mass.: Harvard University Press.

Gingerich, Owen. 1985. "Did Copernicus Owe a Debt to Aristarchus?" *Journal for the History of Astrology* 16 (1): 37–42.

Hameroff, Stuart, and Roger Penrose. 2014. "Consciousness in the Universe: A Review of the 'Orch OR' Theory." *Physics of Life Reviews,* March 11 (1): 39–78.

Harris, Melanie J., N. Chandra Wickramasinghe, David Lloyd, J. V. Narlikar, P. Rajaratnam, Michael P. Turner, Shirwan Al-Mufti, et al. 2002. "Detection of Living Cells in Stratospheric Samples." *Proceedings of SPIE* 4495: 192.

Heilbroner, Robert. 1993. *Twenty-First Century Capitalism.* London: UCL Press Limited, University College.

Henderson, Hazel. 1978. *Creating Alternative Futures: End of Economics.* Princeton, N.J.: Princeton Center for Alternative Futures, Inc.

Hesiod. 1978. *Works and Days.* Japanese translation by Iwanami Shoten. Oxford: Clarendon Press.

Horie, Masayuki, Tomoyuki Honda, Yoshiyuki Suzuki, Yuki Kobayashi, Takuji Daito, Tatsuo Oshida, Kazuyoshi Ikuta, et al. 2010. "Endogenous Non-retroviral RNA Virus Elements in Mammalian Genomes." *Nature* 463: 84–87.

Hoyle, Fred, and N. Chandra Wickramasinghe. 1978a. "Comets, Ice Ages, and Ecological Catastrophes." *Astrophysics and Space Science* 53 (2): 523–26.

———. 1978b. *Lifecloud.* London: J. M. Dent.

———. 1979. *Diseases from Space.* London: J. M. Dent.

———. 1980. *Evolution from Space.* London: J. M. Dent.

———. 1980. *Astrophysics and Space Science* 69: 511.

———. 1981. "Comets—A Vehicle for Panspermia." In *Comets and the Origin of Life,* edited by C. Ponnamperuma, 227. Dordrecht, the Netherlands: D. Reidel.

———. 1982. *Evolution from Space.* London: J. M. Dent.

———. 1985. *Living Comets.* Cardiff, Wales: University College Cardiff Press.

———. 1991. *The Theory of Cosmic Grains.* Dordrecht, the Netherlands: Kluwer Academic Press.

———. 2000. *Astronomical Origins of Life: Steps towards Panspermia.* Dordrecht, the Netherlands: Kluwer Academic Press.

Ikeda, Daisaku, and Chandra Wickramasinghe. 1998. *Space and Eternal Life.* London: Journeyman Press.

Illich, Ivan. 1974. *Energy and Equity: The Right to Useful Unemployment and Its Professional Enemies.* London: Calder & Boyars Ltd.

Kuhn, Thomas S. 1992. *The Copernican Revolution: Planetary Astronomy in the Development of Western Thought.* Cambridge, Mass.: Harvard University Press.

Lakatos, Imre. 1976. *Proofs and Refutations: The Logic of Mathematical*

Discovery. Edited by J. Worrall and E. Zahar. New York: Cambridge University Press.

Locke, John. 1690. *The Two Treaties of Government*. Japanese translation by Iwanami Shoten.

Maddison, Angus. 2001. *The World Economy: A Millennial Perspective*. Paris: Development Center of the Organisation for Economic Co-operation and Development.

Marcus, Gary F., and Simon E. Fisher. 2003. "FOXP2 in Focus: What Can Genes Tell Us about Speech and Language?" *Trends in Cognitive Sciences* 7 (6): 257. http://dx.doi.org/10.1016/S1364-6613(03)00104-9 (accessed October 9, 2018).

Mi, Sha, X. Lee, X. Li, G. M. Veldman, H. Finnerty, L. Racie, E. LaVallie, et al. 2000. "Syncytin Is a Captive Retroviral Envelope Protein Involved in Human Placental Morphogenesis." *Nature* 403: 785–89.

Napier, William M. 2010. "Palaeolithic Extinctions and the Taurid Complex." *Monthly Notices of the Royal Astronomical Society* 405: 1901–6.

The NIH HMP Working Group, Jane Peterson, Susan Garges, Maria Giovanni, Pamela McInnes, Lu Wang, Jeffery A. Schloss, et al. 2009. "The NIH Human Microbiome Project." *Genome Research* 19: 2317–23.

Ossendrijver, Mathieu. 2016. "Ancient Babylonian Astronomers Calculated Jupiter's Position from the Area under a Time-Velocity Graph." *Science* 351: 482–84.

Qin, J., R. Li, J. Raes, M. Arumugam, K. S. Burgdorf, C. Manichanh, T. Nielsen, et al. 2010. "A Human Gut Microbial Gene Catalogue Established by Metagenomic Sequencing." *Nature* 464: 59–65.

Ryan, Frank. 2009. *Virolution*. London: Harper Collins.

Schumacher, Ernest Friedrich. 1973. *Small Is Beautiful*. London: Blond & Briggs Ltd.

Simmel, Georg. 1900. *Philosophies des Geldes*. Japanese translation by Hakusuisha, 1999.

Soddy, Frederic. 1983. *Wealth, Virtual Wealth and Debt: The Solution of the Economic Paradox*. London: George Allen & Unwin Ltd.

Steele, E. J. 2016. In Levin, M., Adams, D. S. (Eds.), *Ahead of the Curve— Hidden Breakthroughs in the Biosciences,* chapter 3. Bristol, UK: Michael Levin and Dany Spencer Adams IOP Publishing Ltd.

Steele, E. J. et al. 2018. "Cause of Cambrian Explosion—Terrestrial or Cosmic?" *Progress in Biophysics and Molecular Biology,* 136, 3–23.

————. 2019. "Mature Extraterrestrial Biology in Astrophysical Phenomena. Reply to Critical numerical analysis of R. Duggleby (2018).

Temple, Robert. 2007. "The Prehistory of Panspermia: Astrophysical or Metaphysical?" *International Journal of Astrobiology* 6 (2): 169–80.

Turnbaugh, Peter J., Ruth E. Ley, Micah Hamady, Claire Fraser-Liggett, Rob Knight, and Jeffrey L. Gordon. 2007. "The Human Microbiome Project: Exploring the Microbial Part of Ourselves in a Changing World." *Nature* 449: 804–810.

Villarreal, Luis P. 2004. "Can Viruses Make Us Human?" *Proceedings of the American Philosophy Society* 148: 296–323.

Wainwright, Milton, N. Chandra Wickramasinghe, J. V. Narlikar, and P. Rajaratnam. 2003. "Microorganisms Cultured from Stratospheric Air Samples Obtained at 41 km." *FEMS Microbiology Letters* 218: 161–65.

Weinstein, L. 1976. "Influenza—1918, a Revisit?" *New England Journal of Medicine* 294: 1058–60.

Wickramasinghe, Chandra. 2001. *Cosmic Dragons: Life and Death on Our Planet.* London: Souvenir Press.

————. 2005. *A Journey with Fred Hoyle.* Singapore: World Scientific Press.

————. 2015. *The Search for Our Cosmic Ancestry.* Singapore: World Scientific Press.

Wickramasinghe, Janaki T., N. Chandra Wickramasinghe, and William M. Napier. 2010. *Comets and the Origin of Life.* Singapore: World Scientific Press.

Wickramasinghe, N. Chandra, and Robert Bauval. 2018. *Cosmic Womb.* Rochester, Vt.: Inner Traditions.

Wickramasinghe, N. Chandra, Ananda Nimalasuriya, Milton Wainwright, and Gensuke Tokoro. 2015. "Microbiome: A Possible Space Component?" *Journal of Astrobiology and Outreach* 3: 139. doi:10.4172/2332-2519.1000139.

Wickramasinghe, N. Chandra, and Gensuke Tokoro. 2014. "Life as a Cosmic Phenomenon: 1. The Socio-Economic Control of a Scientific Paradigm." *Journal of Astrobiology and Outreach* 2: 133.

INDEX

abiogenesis, 26–27

alien gene isolation, 112

Alvarez, Luis and Walter, 81

Anaxoragas, 75, 94

Aquinas, Saint Thomas, 95

Aristarchus of Samos, 60–61, 62

Aristotelean principles, 2, 95–97

Aristotle, 2, 6–8, 95

artificial intelligence, 39, 109

Asoka, King, 79, 100

asteroids, 22, 55, 82, 126. *See also* collisions; comets

Babylonians, 99

Bacon, Francis, 72–73

bacteria. *See also* viruses
    from comets, pandemics and, 15
    cosmic, 2, 9, 126
    most ancient, 21
    new characteristics, 47
    threats of outside source, 103

Baillie, Mike, 89, 90, 91

big bang cosmology, 24, 114

biotechnology, 127

Bondi, Hermann, 114

borna virus, 46–47

Boulding, Kenneth E., 49, 54

Brahe, Tycho, 2, 64

brain-computer analogy, 39

Bruno, Giordano, 2, 65–66, 75–76

Buddha, 75, 76, 77–78, 79, 94, 100, 111

Buddhism, 39–40, 75, 76–77, 79, 100, 105

Buddhist meditation, 40

Buddhist psychology, 40

bunched collisions, 83–84, 88, 90

carbon, 31, 121

carbon-based life forms, 30, 31

chloroplasts, 42–43

Christianity, 75, 76

Clarke, Arthur C., 107–10, 111, 113

"Clarke orbit," 107

Classical Greece, 2, 14–15

collisions. *See also* asteroids; comets
    bunched, 83–84, 88, 90
    civilizations and empires and, 87
    Earth surface temperature and, 85–86
    15,000 years ago, 85
    Great Pyramids and, 89, 90

historical chart, 84
kinetic energy of impact, 86
last ice age and, 85
next date for, 91–92
Old Testament and, 90
risks of, 83
sixty-five million years ago, 126
tidal waves and tsunamis and, 88
tree rings and, 91
Tunguska, 86–88
cometary panspermia, 5
Comet Encke, 83
comets. *See also* collisions
breakup of, 90
Halley's Comet, 11, 12, 73, 110
impacting Earth, 22, 55
life in, 13
microorganisms' arrival via, 71
organic model, 11
spotting in advance, 126
Comet Shoemaker-Levy 9, 82–83
Confucius, 75, 93, 100, 107
conscious mind, 39
consciousness
ancient concepts of, 34–35
in Buddhist psychology, 40
cosmic, 35, 120
existence in its own right, 38
ideas of, 104
levels of interpretation, 34
manifestation of, 104
nature of, 34–41
neurons and, 38
Socratic views of, 35
Copernican revolution, 2, 59–69, 78
Copernicus, Nicolaus, 2, 61–63, 78
copper, 87–88

cosmic connection, 67–68, 122
cosmic consciousness, 35
Cosmic Dragons: Life and Death on Our Planet (Wickramasinghe), 110
cosmic origins
acceptance of, 26
imperfect attempts to interpret, 26
importance of acknowledging, 105
realization of, 103–4
as self-evident, 1, 103
understanding of, 103
ungrudging acceptance of, 111
viruses and bacteria of, 9
"cowboy economy," 54
cultural superiority, 97

Democritus, 75
destiny, control of, 67
disease, 14
DNA, 1, 5, 9, 13, 16, 26–27, 40, 55
DNA sequencing
automated techniques, 44
squid and octopus genomes, 23

Earth-like planets, 19–21
Earth surface temperature, 85–86
economics, 54–55, 56
Egypt, 88–89, 93, 94
Egyptian texts, 97, 100
Einstein, Albert, 36–37, 115
energy expenditure, 52, 53
enlightenment, 120
enzymes, 32
Europa, 113
evolution, 21–22, 51–52
exoplanets, 113–14
extinction of species, 22, 55, 81, 126

extraterrestrial life
  discovery of, 68–69
  search for, 102
  world systems, 78

Fisher, Simon, 46
Fitzgerald, Edward, 25
fossil fuels, 117
fourth dimension, 35–36
FOXP2 gene, 46, 53, 123

Galilei, Galileo, 64–65, 75
gene sequencing, 44, 45, 53, 68
genetic inheritance, 122
genetic modification, 112–13
geocentric universe, 2, 8, 13, 103
Gingerich, Owen, 62
Giotto space probe, 11
global warming, 123
God, 31, 32, 33, 75, 104, 121
Gold, Thomas, 114
Great Pyramids, 89, 90
Greece, 94
greed, 53–54, 56–57
Greetings, Carbon-Based Bipeds!:
  Collected Essays 1934–1998
  (Clarke), 109–10

Hadean epoch, 21
Halley's Comet, 11, 12, 73, 110
Hameroff, Stuart, 38–39
heterodoxy, 4–5
Hinduism, 74, 77, 78–79
Homo erectus, 53
Homo habilis, 53
Homo sapiens, 16, 18, 28, 49, 73
Homo sapiens sapiens, 1, 42–48, 52,

53–54, 55, 83, 91, 120
Horsehead Nebula, 10
Hoyle, Fred, 5–6, 15–17, 31, 66, 71,
  80–81, 97, 114
Hubble, Edwin, 114
human genome technology, 111–12
human gut microbiome, 43–44

ice age, next, 125
India, 99
Indian Space Research Organization
  (ISRO), 71
Indus valley, 99–100
information technology, 124–25
intellectual challenges, 123
intelligence
  emergence of, 121
  superiority of, 27
  supreme, 30–32
intelligent design, 27–28
international belligerence, 105
interstellar organic molecules, 6, 9–10
Islam, 75

Judaism, 75, 76

Kennett, James, 85
Kepler, Johannes, 2, 63–64, 66
Khayam, Omar, 18, 25
Kipling, Rudyard, 70

language, 53
Leibniz, Gottfried von, 73, 99
Lemaître, Georges, 114
life
  carbon-based, 30, 31
  in comets, 13

deepest mystery of, 26
extraterrestrial, 68–69
implications of, 23
informational system, 23–24, 28
intelligent design and, 27–28
multicelled, Cambrian explosion of, 21
origin and evolution, 21–22
respect for, 101
siliceous form of, 28
as superastronomically complex, 9
web of, 2

Malthus, Thomas, 50, 57
microbial protein, 116
microbiology discoveries, 13
microbiomes, 43–45
microorganisms, 2, 13, 43, 71. *See also* bacteria; viruses
military expenditure, 111, 112
military technology, 111
Milky Way, 8, 10, 18, 113
Millay, Vincent, 3
Miller, Stanley, 8–9
Mitchell, Edgar, 41
mitochondria, 42–43
monetary system, 116–17
money, 56
Mycoplasma genitalium, 27

nature, harmony with, 120
neurons, 38, 39
Newton, Isaac, 2, 66, 99, 115
Newton's theory of gravitation, 73
nuclear fission, 117
nuclear war, 127

Oparin-Haldane theory, 6, 8
organic comet model, 11
organic molecules
  in comets, 13
  formation from inorganic chemicals, 8
  formation in early Earth's atmosphere, 8–9
  interstellar, 6, 9–10
orthodoxy, 4
oxygen, 31

pandemics, 14–15, 17, 103, 125–26, 127
Pasteur, Louis, 95–96, 121
Penrose, Roger, 38–39, 104
Philolaus of Croton, 60, 62
Plague of Justinian, 15
plagues, 14–15
planets
  Earth-like, 19–21, 105
  knowing position of, 124
  orbiting distant stars, 19, 20
plant seeds, 2, 14
Plato, 35, 75, 94
pollution, 50, 52
primordial soup, 6, 8, 24
prokaryotes, 42
Proxima Centauri, 21, 114

quantum theory, 37
quarks, 115

radiation, 51
religion, 25–26, 39, 73, 75–79, 102, 121, 122
retroviruses, 16, 45–46, 47
Rig Veda, 35, 36

RNA, 9, 27, 45, 55
robots, 29, 30, 39, 125
Rosetta space probe, 13
Rosetta stone, 97, 98
rule of survival, 54

Schrödinger, Erwin, 37–38
Schumacher, Ernst Friedrich, 55
self, 35
SETI, 102
silicon, 28, 29, 30
Silk Route, 71
Socrates, 75, 94
solar energy, 117–18
Spaceguard project, 126–27
"spaceship economy," 54–55
space travelers, 2, 4
Spanish flu pandemic, 15
string theory, 37
Sun worship, 74
superintelligence, 31
syncytin, 45

tardigrades, 14
telepathy, 40–41
theory of cosmic life, 14
trade routes, 70–71
TRU (trans-uranic waste), 50–51
Tunguska, Siberia, 86–88
Turok, Neil, 114–15
2010, Clarke's predictions about, 109
2020, Clarke's predictions about, 109
2030, Clarke's predictions about, 109,
    113
2040, Clarke's predictions about, 109
2050, Clarke's predictions about, 109
2090, Clarke's predictions about, 110

2100 world
    alien gene isolation, 112
    as benchmark, 110–11
    Clarke's predictions, 110
    cosmological models and,
        114–15
    genetic modification, 112–13
    human population, 115–16
    poverty as alleviated, 116
    societal cohesion, 119
    solar energy, 117–18
    "space drive," 110
    space eyes, 113
    travel in, 116

unity, preserving, 102
"universal replicator," 109
Urey, Harold, 8–9

Villarreal, Luis, 48
viral sequences, 16
viruses. *See also* bacteria
    borna, 46–47
    comet-borne, 68
    from comets, pandemics and, 15
    cosmic, 9, 52, 126
    Le group, 56
    Lu group, 56
    new characteristics, 47
    objective as replication, 55
    threats of outside source, 103
    Zika, 47–48

Weinstein, Louis, 15–16
Wigner, Eugene, 37

Zika virus, 47–48

BOOKS OF RELATED INTEREST

Cosmic Womb
The Seeding of Planet Earth
by Chandra Wickramasinghe, Ph.D., and Robert Bauval

Black Genesis
The Prehistoric Origins of Ancient Egypt
by Robert Bauval and Thomas Brophy, Ph.D.

Origins of the Sphinx
Celestial Guardian of Pre-Pharaonic Civilization
by Robert M. Schoch, Ph.D., and Robert Bauval

Forgotten Civilization
The Role of Solar Outbursts in Our Past and Future
by Robert M. Schoch, Ph.D.

Lost Knowledge of the Ancients
A Graham Hancock Reader
Edited by Glenn Kreisberg

The Great Pyramid Hoax
The Conspiracy to Conceal the True History of Ancient Egypt
by Scott Creighton
Foreword by Laird Scranton

Forbidden History
Prehistoric Technologies, Extraterrestrial Intervention,
and the Suppressed Origins of Civilization
Edited by J. Douglas Kenyon

DNA of the Gods
The Anunnaki Creation of Eve and the Alien Battle for Humanity
by Chris H. Hardy, Ph.D.

INNER TRADITIONS BEAR & COMPANY
Rochester, VT 05767
1-800-246-8648
www.innertraditions.com

Or contact your local bookseller